CAPSIZE!

A Story of Survival in the North Atlantic

CAPSIZE!

A Story of Survival in the North Atlantic

by Nicolas Angel

with a preface by **Alain Bombard**

translated from the original French
by **Alan Wakeman**

W · W · NORTON & COMPANY
New York   London

Library of Congress Cataloging in Publication Data

Angel, Nicolas, 1954–
    Capsize! a story of survival in the North
Altantic.

    Translation of Chavirage en trimaran R.T.L.-
Timex.
    Published in 1980 under title: Capsize in a
trimaran.
    1. RTL-Timex (Ship)   2. Survival (after air-
plane accidents, shipwrecks, etc.)   3. Atlantic
Ocean.   I. Title.
G530.R17A5313   1981   910'.0916348   81–389
ISBN 0–393–03264–7   AACR1

W. W. Norton & Company, Inc. 500 Fifth Avenue, New York, N.Y. 10110
W. W. Norton & Company Ltd. 25 New Street Square, London EC4A 3NT

1 2 3 4 5 6 7 8 9 0

Contents

Preface

Wrecked! The term itself is synonymous with catastrophy: the wreck of a family, of a life, of a personality!

But wrecked at sea – the association of two terrible words, one situational, the other elemental. Wrecked at sea – who hasn't had such a nightmare! In any case it is always present in the consciousness of anyone who sets foot on board ship.

Suddenly the comfortable, safe, orderly everyday world dissolves and in its place is the abrupt contact between naked humanity and the uncontrolled elements. It's no longer just a matter of living, but of surviving! Until 1952, the year of my Atlantic experiment, only airmen and sailors of the Second World War had any real chance of survival. Rescues were organized for them because they were specialists who were expensive to train and difficult to replace. It wasn't the men that had to be saved, but the chosen individuals that time and money had made more precious than *homo simplex*, the man in the street.

It was to this *homo communis* that I wished to give a hope and a technique. Search techniques were perfected from the experiments of the French navy. The liferaft became a necessity. But all that was twenty-seven years ago, and in twenty-seven years the liferaft may have become normal equipment but no spectacular improvements have increased the chances of the shipwrecked.

Thus Nicolas Angel had to confront, in 1979, being shipwrecked in 1953. It's as if one were still flying with Lindbergh's plane today. Nicolas endured the same anguish as me, and ran the same risks.

He wanted to describe his experiences so that life-saving appliances can be improved to further the chances of castaways. That's why I believe this book will save thousands of lives, and I said to him 'Your suffering has not been in vain. I helped to save your life: you will help to ease the lives of others who suffer the same fate, and thereby force the retreat of the curse attached to this terrible word – shipwrecked!'
THANK YOU.

Alain Bombard

CAPSIZE!

A Story of Survival in the North Atlantic

1

The Idea of Being an Example, and Preparations

'D id you know I had a French name? Lemieux, Norman Lemieux. It's a pity you're not staying longer. You could have told me your story in detail and I could have organized a party in your honour.'

I've hardly met the driver of the little bus hired by the Gulf Oil Company and already I'm inundated with questions:

'You must've been bloody freezing!'

'Which one of you started to die?'

'Did you see any sharks?'

I've taken the seat next to him while Olivier, Alain and Denis have a seat each and stretch themselves out. In the absence of real sleep, they can at least doze. I'd like to do the same but I don't want to leave the driver alone, and then I must speak to a 'landlubber'.

Norman Lemieux is the first 'non-sailor' that I've met since our departure from Bermuda. It seems that 'Jaws' or 'Battles in the Pacific' are the only sea stories he's heard till now so that the least detail of our adventures brings sighs of admiration, or more questions like: 'I don't know if I could have stood it, personally, but you're young; what about him?', nodding his head towards the car in front where Alain Gliksman is riding with an American journalist and a Gulf Oil captain.

The miles slip by and after an hour and a half of rapt attention and questions Norman seems content. Then he begins on his own adventures. Knocking with his fist on his right leg as if it were a door, he announces as if it were the most natural thing in the world that he has an artificial leg. Pulling aside the collar of his shirt, he uncovers a long scar at the base of his neck:

'I was twenty. The leg was a grenade, the neck was five minutes later when the Viet Cong tried to finish me off with a bayonet... I had to kill him.... So, 'they' put a guard on me for three months.'

While Norman is telling me of his life as a prisoner of the Vietminh, then of his six months of operations before he could go back to his interrupted life as a student, I start feeling really silly with my account of nine days on a liferaft: it isn't exactly a tragedy. I wonder how he could even interest himself in our little adventure and worry about our health.

I start asking myself a whole lot of questions about the value of this ordeal and what importance one should give it. Until this moment it hadn't occurred to me that this human experience could move anyone but those close to us, least of all people who had suffered like this driver. I was ready to forget the terrifying sound of the waves, to forget the hours, the days spent bailing out the icy water that invaded our craft, to forget the silent fear of the moment when we caught sight of the fins of killer whales. To forget also the times when we cursed who-ever had fitted out our rubber raft.

So, it was only on this highway in Delaware, during the 120 miles between the oil terminal and the city of Philadelphia, that I became aware of the human interest of our story. After all, hadn't our greatest anguish, during the acutest moments of despair in the middle of the Atlantic, been the thought of disappearing without trace? No one would have known how we had died. Alain Gliksman had been obsessed with leaving a message to explain our deaths.

This is why I suddenly stop listening to the driver in this American minibus, and all the images of those nine days which I had been forcing myself to forget run through my mind like a film, making me shiver retrospectively. A little later, in the Gulf Oil clinic in Philadelphia, the sight of our last two vitamin biscuits confirms my task as a witness, and the possible interest in my evidence. In fact it seems unbelievable to me that Alain Gouedard, six feet tall and built like an icebox, could have kept going with these little enriched 'snacks' whereas only five days earlier, in the 'bib'*, having to eat only a quarter seemed as natural as swallowing a steak at lunchtime in a Paris restaurant.

As a journalist, what probably finally convinces me, rather than Olivier, Denis and the two Alains, is finding myself on the other side of the fence. The interviewer interviewed, as it were! At times in this clinic, I no longer know which side I'm on. I ought, rather, to be interviewing the Vietnam war veteran Norman Lemieux. But no, French Television, *Paris Match*, Associated Press and the Gamma Agency have all come for Alain and Denis Gliksman, Olivier Redkine, Alain Gouedard and Nicolas Angel. Yet to their questions, and their astonishment, we reply that they would have reacted the same in our place. The will to live pushes human limits to undreamed-of extremes.

A bit later, still in this same clinic, I'm almost ashamed. The medical examination has at last begun

---

*'Bib' is short for Bibendum, the Michelin Tyre Company's publicity character, who appears to be made of inflated rubber tubes.

and stripped to the waist on the scales, I hear myself announcing that I weigh 62 kilos (136 pounds) namely only 3 kilos (6 pounds) less than before my departure. Lemieux is helping with the 'weighing' and it's getting to be an obsession: I imagine him in the same situation after his liberation; I imagine his impressive thinness. To have lost 6 pounds after such an adventure is almost ridiculous: for pity's sake, I was hoping to have lost at least 40. He says nothing, and unlike the journalists present goes off discreetly to wait for us outside. We're not told the results of this medical, but judging by the relaxed state of the doctor we understand that all is well. We're all suffering from burns and skin irritations due to the seawater, and as far as Alain Gliksman is concerned rather more serious nervous exhaustion. The press is frustrated in its desire for spectacular symptoms, but we're relieved not to find ourselves in hospital beds for a period of observation.

Denis doesn't forget to pay tribute to the crew of the *Afran Dawn* (the Gulf Oil Liberian-registered tanker which rescued us) and the talents of its cook who virtually gave us intravenous shots of spaghetti for three days.

Olivier, who at the moment of rescue was in the worst state of all of us, bursts out laughing when he learns that his weight hasn't changed by so much as a gram since our departure.

Then an evening, and the welcome of the French Consul in Philadelphia helps us to forget those nine days. But the next morning, jumping out of bed after a night of light sleep, albeit without dreams or nightmares for the first time, the ground's moving! Wide awake and I am – we all are – back on that bloody raft. This pitching feeling on awakening takes a whole week to disappear completely.

Strangely, during all these nights that followed our

rescue we stopped dreaming; perhaps we did dream, but we could no longer remember it. Maybe we'd used up our stock of dreams in the middle of the Atlantic.

Before joining Alain Gliksman and his 'monsters' (as he called Denis, Olivier and Alain) I had dreamed of *RTL-Timex.* I had known nothing more about her than the photos in the yachting press at the time of the Route du Rhum race.* Among the papers that I'd left at Radio-Television Luxembourgeois before my departure, I had described this trimaran as an 'immense sea spider', and for a week before leaving for Bermuda my nights were haunted by the image of this 'spider'. I could already see myself at Deauville, my face tanned, mangy with an eight day beard, the Atlantic crossing record-beater, welcomed by his mates, mainly journalists from RTL, RMC and so on.... There was no doubt whatever in my mind that, with Alain Gliksman and his team, we would make Lizard Point, to the extreme southwest of Cornwall, from New York, in less than 12 days, 4 hours and 1 minute. I, who was always talking about sailing as if I'd spent my whole life on a ketch, was finally going to realize my dream, and in the most spectacular way possible. Those who thought I was a 'Charlie' and that my adventures at sea would never happen outside my own head – well, they'd see! Yuk!

Originally it wasn't planned that a journalist from Radio Luxembourg should be on board *RTL-Timex.* There was supposed to be a woman colleague from *L'Express* and a man from *L'Equipe,* but RTL wasn't to be represented. When we heard this Roger Zabel from

---

*A race for singlehanded monohulls and multihulls, from St Malo in Brittany to Pointe a Pitre, Guadaloupe in November 1979. The event was organized by the French shortly after it was announced that the Royal Western Y.C./Observer Singlehanded Transatlantic Race (OSTAR) would in future limit the size of competing boats, and, as was the intention, attracted a number of large and unusual boats.

the sports service and I couldn't believe our ears. We spent a whole evening using every trick in the book to persuade Alain Gliksman that a boat called *RTL* could not, without ridicule, go to sea without one of our journalists on board. That's why, three days later, Alain Gliksman informed the representative of *L'Équipe* that I was going instead of him. He must have been disappointed at the time, but now he's probably congratulating himself on his narrow escape.

A week later Alain went off to collect his boat from the Îles des Saintes, near Guadaloupe, where his son Denis, Alain Gouedard and Olivier Redkine, all professional crew, were waiting for him. They had been working like slaves for twelve weeks to repair the damage suffered by the boat, then named *Seiko*, during the Route du Rhum. Alain had been unable to finish this race because of bad weather in the Gulf of Gascony, but also, I should add, he was particularly handicapped by damage to the port float, which was taking on water. He had to give up in the Azores and it was there that Denis, Alain 2 and Olivier took over to sail her to Guadeloupe. It was the same trio who had prepared the trimaran on the eve of the French transatlantic crossing.

The deck layout was particularly poor. Derek Kelsall and Nick Keig, designer and builder of the boat (as *Three Legs of Mann II*) had provided ridiculously feeble rigging and under-sized fittings. Despite the light rigging, it was on this trimaran that President Jimmy Carter sailed with his wife and his daughter Amy between two sessions of the Guadeloupe summit conference. Then it was a matter of cruising, not ocean racing. To prepare for the record attempt, *Seiko* had been drydocked and pampered by the 'monsters'. Scraped, sanded, painted, repainted, light winches replaced. The floats above all had been coated and recoated to prevent the tiniest drop of water from entering. All stays and chainplates, which until then had been attached direct to the foam-sandwich polyester hull, had been reinforced. So *Seiko*, become *RTL-Timex*, had changed her skin during three months of strenuous work in a little yard down a creek of the Saintes.

When Alain Gliksman returned from Paris where he'd been sorting out money problems and refinancing the boat, he could hardly recognize the freshly repainted sky-blue and white trimaran. All that remained was to stick on the letters of the new name: *RTL* on the main hull, *Timex* on the floats.

Between the Iles des Saintes and Bermuda, where I was to join them, Gliksman and his team indulged in the pleasure of participating in the first stage of the Trade Wind Race, which attracts all the finest boats from this part of the Atlantic, notably that king of multihull yachts *Rogue Wave*, skippered by Philip Weld – a trimaran that wins almost every race. The *RTL-Timex* crew were first past practically every mark and won this stage, after time adjustments, having jammed their speedometer at a water speed estimated at 25 knots at times. The arrival at Sint-Marteen, the western and Dutch part of the island of Saint-Martin, confirmed the boat's competitiveness.

Walking past a shipchandler's shop that day, Alain Gliksman stopped short in front of a piece of radio equipment: an American-made distress beacon that isn't approved by the French authorities. In case of emergencies it can transmit on civil aviation frequencies, and thus be picked up by the first airline in the vicinity. Gliksman looked at the price and hesitated. 'Better wait till we get to New York,' he said. 'It'll cost less and I'll have time to connect it up.'

In Paris on Thursday, March 29, I'm stuck in a

1st set of waves
from warm front.

2nd set of waves
from cold front:
the waves cross
and break.

M.Gilles

hopeless traffic jam due to an accident on the ring road. My plane for St George's Island in Bermuda via London is at 08.10 and at 07.40 my taxi is somewhere between the Porte Dauphine and the Porte Maillot, moving a metre every three minutes. By the time I arrive at Roissy Airport the plane for London has flown and I have to put back my departure for Bermuda. By good or bad luck there's another flight for Bermuda from London the following day, but then nothing for a week. If I miss that one I'll just have to join the crew of *RTL-Timex* in New York like my colleague from *L'Express*. Back at the RTL office, there are guffaws: 'Come on, grab the chance and refuse to go', or the usual skeptical: 'Why not go and see Colas*. . .'.

I take advantage of this extra day to leave last-minute instructions: 'Don't worry, you'll have a report every three days. But if I don't manage to get in contact, try calling by Radio St-Lys. You can do it at night, there's less interference.'

I can't sleep much during my last night in my bed. So instead I go over my lessons like a good little crew member. I learn by heart how to gybe the spinnaker with one or two poles. I check to see if I've left anything out of my sea bag. Boots, oilskins, pullovers, a lucky charm given me by my best girlfriend, an arctic anorak for sailing above the fiftieth parallel, gloves, glasses – everything's there. I go back to bed and nap for an hour. A quick warm-up when I jump out of bed confirms that my training sessions during the last four weeks haven't

---

*A reference to Alain Colas, who had failed to arrive at Guadaloupe in the Route du Rhum. His aluminium trimaran *Manureva*, a boat which he had raced and sailed singlehanded for many thousands of miles, was the object of an air search but has never been sighted. As Colas was known to have carried only a limited supply of a vital medicine, required because of the after-effects of a severe leg injury, there is an additional element of doubt as to the cause of his death and the loss of his boat.

been a waste of time. And finally I leave, deciding this time to go by *Métro* and train to catch the plane. I arrive in the nick of time at the check-in, but I don't miss *this* plane!

It's six days since *RTL-Timex* left Sint-Marteen. She should have arrived at St George's Island already, but she's hit a depression and headwinds that force her to beat and hence slow her down. On board, Denis, Olivier and the two Alains joke, 'Hardly surprising, we're in the middle of the Bermuda Triangle.'

It isn't even possible to console themselves with a good meal because Denis, who was in charge of stores, short-sightedly laid on a feast before the departure, and all that's left is some cabbage and a few tins of sweetcorn. So this will be their lunch and dinner menu until they arrive.

At St George's, having disentangled myself from the local immigration authorities, my first thought is to go to the yacht harbour. No *RTL-Timex*, so I go off to the maritime radio station, built on a hillside out of stones from an old castle, to see what I can find out. No boat of this name has docked at Bermuda recently. However, the operator can try calling her, if I know the details and if she's near enough to pick up VHF. This first attempt, and subsequent ones, prove fruitless. Nothing to do but leave the number of my St George's guesthouse, so that he can telephone me as soon as he has any news.

A message comes the first night, but not the one I'd hoped for, since it's from Paris and makes my landlady angry. She's been woken up three times, at three, four and five o'clock in the morning, by Roger Zabel and my father who, forgetting the time difference, want to tell me that Alain has informed them that because of headwinds he won't be at St George's before Sunday night.

The news leaves me all the time in the world for tourism. My camera gets crammed with the mad colours of Bermudan houses, but Sunday comes and still no message. The operator consults his lists and confirms that there are two French yachts in the vicinity, but neither of them is *RTL-Timex*. The first is *Bel Espoir* and the second *Rara Avis*. What pretty names! Even prettier considering that I know them, as all who love sailing know them: They're the three-masters run by Père Jaouen, also known as 'Le Père' or simply 'Michel'. The priest of the oceans is arriving from the Antilles with his odd crew of young junkies, old-timers and ex-officers of the merchant navy. The operator asks if I know them. Just think, less than five months ago I was supposed to go on board *Bel Espoir* to cover the Route du Rhum. I'd met Le Père at the RTL bar and everyone had agreed except my bosses. In the meantime, Le Père Jaouen had rescued Marc Pajot, an unlucky competitor in this French Transatlantic race, whose 22.5 metre catamaran *Paul Ricard* had begun to sink. Generally speaking we journalists of the spoken word really appreciated Le Père Jaouen because his ship's radio served us as a sort of relay station with the race competitors. This time I can make use of it too, and by the intermediary of Radio Bermuda I ask him if he's seen *RTL-Timex* recently and if he can try to contact Gliksman. The reply is back in no time: 'No sight of *RTL-Timex*', and a few hours later, 'No radio contact.' I resign myself to spending another night in an ordinary bed.

At six o'clock on Monday morning I have a brutal awakening: my terrifying landlady is screaming through the door 'Radio Bermuda just called you: your boat has arrived!'

In less time than it takes to write it, I'm up, dressed, helmeted and have my foot down on the little motorbike I've hired. For three weeks I've pictured myself at the helm of *RTL-Timex*, talked about her to anyone who'd listen, described her as if I'd built her myself. She haunts my dreams. I only live for her and now she's there, like my first electric train under the Christmas tree. I imagine her like a spider on the dawn calm waters of the tiny port of St George's.

Her sails are furled, her floats touch the water in slow motion. Really I want just to stand and stare but Alain Gliksman comes out of the cabin, sees me and shouts 'So, what kept you?' Olivier, Alain and Denis, who I'm seeing for the first time, are sitting, their appearance haggard and hair unruly, with their legs dangling over the edge of the quay. All three have put on their quilted red down 'softies', arctic anoraks which were given to us in Paris. I get off my motorbike, take off my helmet and go over to shake hands. They don't get up: they're obviously exhausted or even half asleep. As I took the precaution of getting descriptions of my future crewmates before leaving, I hardly need the introductions from Gliksman; I feel I almost know them already. Alain Gouedard is the first to finally get up and give me a firm hand; his 'Hallo' is like a burst of laughter, and this is how he continues. His optimism is disarming, and it is what has brought him through all his hard times. At the age of eight he was already winning regattas between Deauville and Houlgate in Normandy with his brother. His father and perhaps more importantly his grandfather have given him a love of sailing and the sea. Sometimes this love practically turns into madness: in 1978 he did a solo crossing of the English Channel in his Hobie cat in force 6 winds.

When Alain sets foot on land it's only to find another boat, which never takes him more than three days. Physically as well as morally he's a natural force. For him everything is 'great': in the worst possible moments he always finds something in the situation which is 'great'.

I sometimes get the impression that Gliksman, who's forty-six, is reassured by the competence and self-assurance of Alain Gouedard, who's only twenty-four. But on this Monday morning Alain Gouedard, like the others, finds it 'great' that we should go and have a big breakfast. So I become their guide and take them off to one of the three tables of the only coffee-shop that's open at 7.30 in the morning on St George's.

Denis Gliksman, white as a sheet till now, gets his colour back. His angel face looks even younger because of a halo of blond curls. At twenty-two he's the crew's favourite. When he's not at sea he's a press photographer, following in his father's footsteps, straddling the worlds of the yachting press and ocean racing. He no longer even thinks how lucky he is to have such a life. His knowledge of sailing and the sea are already impressive, and *RTL-Timex* holds no secrets for him, which is why he thinks of nothing but his future boat. Denis has come to a turning-point in his life as a sailor: after this record attempt he'll no longer be his father's or someone else's crew but skipper of a boat, hopefully his own and to be a trimaran which he's already designing.

After breakfast the crew can only think of a hot shower. Half an hour later they've all caught up on the latest Paris gossip and had their wish: hot water runs in floods. The four tramps I met two hours earlier become an ocean racing crew again, and talk turns to technical matters concerned with the small changes needed to perfect the boat.

Olivier Redkine is probably the most secretive of all. He seems less integrated into the team, probably because he was the last to join. He's twenty-four too. Like the others, his only interest for years has been the sea, but he doesn't proclaim it so loudly. Born in Anjou, he has the gentleness that poets speak of, but also he is discrete under duress, covering up his joy, fear and sometimes even his sadness. It's a quality that could cost him his life.

The stopover at St George's Island was supposed to be for two days but gets extended to four. On a thoroughbred like *RTL-Timex* the crew are always finding extra little fine adjustments to make. While Alain Gliksman is on the telephone to Paris negotiating the purchase of two new boats to add to his stable, we sand and fill the hull as much to give our trimaran the maximum efficiency as to assist in manoeuvring and reduce the risk of accidents or simply to improve our comfort.

These four days change my attitude and that of the others in my regard. I'm no longer just a journalist invited to accompany them but a crew member, less of an old hand than the rest but a member of the team who will have his role to play in this attempt to beat the seventy-four year old transatlantic sailing record of the American schooner *Atlantic*. My only disappointment during these four days is to learn that on a trimaran you don't need poles to set a spinnaker. Apparently the operation is easier than on a monohulled vessel, but this was exactly where I'd hoped to demonstrate my greatest skill!

On Wednesday April 4 the sky is as blue as ever over Bermuda and I'm putting the finishing touches to the portholes to make them perfectly watertight. At last I feel completely at home on the boat. Olivier and Alain 2 (Gouedard) are arranging the food stores and lash a case of wine under the step to the rear cabin. Alain, as usual between two roars of laughter, shouts to me 'At least we'll have some booze if we have to spend some time in the capsule'; seeing my puzzled expression, he adds, 'the survival capsule'. So there's a space designed as a survival capsule as on Alain Colas' boat! For me this news is both worrying and reassuring. I'd like to know more about this aspect of the trimaran, but I don't risk asking questions for fear that my words will get interpreted as a form of disquiet. However, I willingly have a look at this 'capsule' out of simple curiosity to see what it's like and how one gets into it. Is it for only one person? Do you get in from forward or aft? What is it like inside?

At 3.30 p.m. the wind gets up. Denis has just dismantled the port winch to clean and grease it. Alain 2 is coiling the anchor warp. Olivier has finished organizing the galley. Thanks to his talents as a chef, he must often be asked to do lunch and dinner parties, and he knows it. As for me, I'm using my charm on the owner of a restaurant to get hold of two blocks of ice, to keep the butter and yoghurts fresh, the latter being Alain Gouedard's one vice.

Alain Gliksman, who's just come back from the meteorological station of the American military base at St George's Island, writes in his log 'No need to wait any longer, everyone's ready to leave this afternoon.'

2

Flipped Like a Pancake

F or two hours we've been laughing our heads
off, it's so unbelievable. Our departure from St
George's deserves to be in the annals of ocean racing
history. Gliksman is exultant: 'I'd give a lot to see
Karsauson's face if we manage a flying start like that
from New York....' Personally, I still haven't got my
breath back. About 4.30, while Denis was reassembling
the mainsheet winch, which he'd just greased, his father
was running up to the end of the quay. To make a safe
departure we had to avoid a sandbank and an enormous buoy, so we decided to move the boat along the
quay a hundred metres. Like many ocean yachts *RTL-
Timex* has no engine, so Alain is fixing a warp to enable
us to haul her up to the end of the quay. Meanwhile
Olivier and Denis are putting up the mainsail while
Alain 2 has thrown a rope to the owner of the coffee-
shop, who's closed to help us with our departure. He
won't be disappointed. The instant the sail is up *RTL-
Timex* takes off, tearing the mooring line out of his hands
and hurtling off like a virtual rocket, leaving the twenty
or so spectators who've come to see us off, flabber-
gasted. So we slip into the tiny pass of St George's Bay.

On the way through, Alain shows us the rock where, a month earlier, another helmsman with the same type of trimaran came to grief.

It gets cooler, the sun touches the horizon and the wind begins to strengthen. After three hours' sailing it's reached force 6 or 7 and the waves are a bit bigger. For the fifth time I'm asked if I'm O.K., if I feel all right. Of course I feel all right – I'm in a dream. I'm about to spend my first night on the high seas out of sight of land; it's Nirvana. So Gouedard explains that it's always difficult to get your sea legs with a trimaran, even for old hands. After leaving the Azores none of the three crew had been able to swallow a thing for three days. My four companions have already had a secret meeting, though I won't hear about it till four days later, and reached the unanimous decision that to keep my hands and brain occupied it would be a good idea to let me take the helm. The course to keep is 330°, i.e. between 30° and 40° to the apparent wind. Between these limits I have leeway: one must struggle to keep the sails from flapping. I wasn't expecting to take the helm so soon, but I accept without too much persuasion, remarking 'You obviously like taking risks.'

After half an hour's plain sailing, Alain decides to reduce canvas. The wind is reaching 35 to 40 knots at times. While I'm doing my best to maintain course, Denis and Alain 2 take down the staysail and tie two reefs in the mainsail. Concentrating on maintaining course has given me a headache. A glance at the compass, a glance at the mainsail, a glance at the compass, a glance at the mainsail.... The figures turn, settle down. The foam on the waves becomes phosphorescent in the night and suddenly I don't feel very well. After an hour of this routine, I can't stand it anymore. My legs are like jelly and I have a strong desire to throw my lunchtime meal overboard. The plate of mashed sausage that Olivier offers me from inside the cabin is the last straw. I hand over my place, the helm, the course and plunge into the cabin where I collapse onto the only free bunk. My first night will be a calvary punctuated by spasms of vomiting, continuing long after my stomach is empty. Once, at 3 o'clock in the morning, my pride will get the upper hand and I shall demand to do my watch like the others. But again the compass, the sail, the sail, the compass, and a few good showers of icy water all over the cockpit will bring me to the end of my willpower. I finish the night in the sail locker, curled up on the spinnaker bag.

When I stick my nose out at dawn this Thursday, Denis is at the helm and his father has turned on the VHF to talk to the U.S. Coast Guard, whose frigate is following a course parallel to ours.

'Coast Guard from *RTL-Timex*. Good morning.'

'*Timex* from Coast Guard. Good morning! Everything O.K.?'

'We are all right, thank you.'

'*Timex* from Coast Guard. Where are you from and where are you bound?'

'We are going from St George's, Bermuda. And we are going to New York.'

'*Timex* from Coast Guard. Thank you, and have a good trip.'

A brief enough conversation, but the appearance of this ship irritates me. Obviously, if the Coast Guard is still in the area it's because we aren't very far from the coast. I share this thought with Alain, who assures me that despite our reduced sail we have covered a hundred or so miles during the night. He adds, 'Without appearing to, they were checking up on us. There's a lot of drug trafficking on yachts in this area.'

'Checking up?'

'Yes. If we don't arrive in New York, but in Miami or elsewhere, the boat will be suspected.'

I've become completely dehydrated during my painful night and a glass of water would be welcome. I hesitate, hardly daring to swallow anything for fear of having to lean overboard yet again. Alain Gouedard, who's just come on watch, advises me to eat and drink whatever the consequences. I'd prefer to go and lie down again as I don't feel too strong on my legs. It's at this point that Alain says sympathetically, 'Come on, don't worry. In another twenty-four to forty-eight hours it'll all be over.' The mere thought of another twenty-four hours in this state makes me tremble. So I decide on the spot that I'm *not* ill! I stay in the cockpit and start chatting with Alain. I'm determined to talk about everything and nothing, and stop thinking about retching and stomachache. Half an hour later I feel well enough to eat an orange. No sooner eaten than spewed up. Never mind, I'm going to show these pros I can take it.

Alain has understood my desire to seem and become useful again. He starts explaining the finer points of helming in terms of broaching waves. *RTL-Timex* skids slightly backwards as she unfalteringly climbs these waves, which sometimes reach eight metres in height. It's a bit like the controlled skid of a car on a snow-covered road. The port float hardly touches the water. From time to time it crashes against the crest of a breaking wave and the repercussive shock runs through the whole hull. The wind is getting more and more violent and it smashes the crests, preventing the waves from breaking along their whole length. Gliksman is still bent over the chart table. Roughly every three hours he turns on the radio receiver to listen to and note down the Coast Guard weather bulletins. He taps the barometer mechanically from time to time – it's beginning to fall heavily. An hour before our departure the needle was at 1014 millibars, this morning it's below 1010. Muffled up in my oilskins, I spend some of my watch seated on the 'bib' which is lashed beneath the wheel. It's useful to sit on, but the liferaft in its plastic case is a bit in the way when it comes to trimming the mainsail or steering while standing up. I often stumble into it or climb up on it without ever thinking of its actual purpose. The end of the mainsheet slider is jammed between the raft and the after cabin bulkhead. In freeing it Denis has it in mind to lash the raft more securely, but this means waiting for the weather to calm. Which it doesn't. On the contrary, the wind is getting stronger and stronger and the sea carries more and more impressive waves. As dusk falls, Gliksman leaves his chart table and comes out like the devil from hell, crying: 'I don't believe it! They're still forecasting winds of 20 knots when we've already got 30 and the barometer's falling!'

Five minutes later he decides to lower the mainsail, which Denis and Olivier stow on the boom.

The crew's getting organized; watches are shared out without problems. Because of the bad weather, and to get us used to the rhythm we'll use during the race, he orders two men per four hour watch. I share my watch with Gouedard, which suits me for the simple reason that we fit together. Alain 2's competence and self-assurance make a better teacher of him than the others (except Gliksman). Although he's a sailor to the roots of his hair, he knows how to use clear language. And his apparent nonchalance reassures me; I don't see and I don't feel his gaze aimed at my every movement, but I know he's behind me, ready to prevent any fatal mistake. And I make plenty of mistakes, that night, so that for Alain the watches are twice as exhausting than if he was alone. A succession of gusts cause me to round up suddenly three times, and three times Alain rushes up onto the foredeck to help the staysail around the mast when we tack. Between times he comes to check our heading. To prevent myself from falling asleep when I'm not at the helm, I use the hand pump to empty out any water that may have got into the floats. The repairs carried out in Guadaloupe make it an easy business. Originally there were three hand pumps, one for the main hull and one for each float. Moreover they had to be moved from left to right at calf-height: naval architects should try pumping more often! The main hull pump is now electric, and those for the two floats have been combined. I can pump up and down, comfortably seated on the cockpit bench, so when my arm's tired all I have to do is lean back. It's a small detail which saves us time and energy. During the night, the last hour of the watch seems as long as the three previous ones. We are numbed by the cold, the damp penetrates our oilskins, fatigue remains the most trying sensation and sleep creeps up on us. I notice that Alain's head is nodding slowly backwards and for-wards, then suddenly his chin touches his chest and this uncontrolled movement wakes him up. The end of the watch is like a deliverance. Orders are soon passed: 'Careful, the wind's variable. If it turns a bit, keep to 270°. As to canvas, don't hesitate to increase the stay-sail a bit if it weakens. We're not making much headway.'

Before closing the hatch, Alain, who's just joined me in the stern cabin, shouts to our replacements 'Have fun, might see you tomorrow!'

Before even taking our oilskins off, our first action is to shove a cassette on the stereo and put the kettle on. Then we take our boots and oilskin trousers off. Outside in the cockpit, the movements of the boat aren't worrying; inside they turn us into ninepins. Exactly as with the wheel, one must anticipate the wave movements in order not to be thrown over. This is a trying business, but give it another four days and I'll never forget it. Alain's made some toast to go with our honey tea. Thanks to this light snack and the musical accompaniment, we can practically forget that we're in the middle of the raging Atlantic. Who was it told me before leaving that life aboard a trimaran was appalling? My seasickness has completely disappeared. Alain is pleasantly surprised at this because he feared having a virtual corpse on his hands for three days. I keep just a tee-shirt on and slip into the sleeping bag, still warm from its previous occupant. With an automatic gesture Alain shoves another cassette into the tape deck fixed over his head – a recording of Billie Joel, his favourite singer. My eyes close. I only open them two or three times when a wave breaks over the hull and shakes my bunk.

Three and a half hours later, Olivier's shaking me. I've slept like a baby. The desire to stay in my sleeping bag is intense, but I remember a discussion I had with Gliksman a month earlier in Paris. We were talking about life on board a yacht during an ocean race and I was saying how lucky I was not to have to go with Olivier de Kersauson because, according to reports I'd heard, this 'tyrant' thought nothing of waking his crew up by kicking them. To my great surprise Gliksman replied, 'Of course. So what. If the crew aren't keen,they need a shock.' On this Friday morning, the memory of that little conversation has me on my feet in no time.

No improvement outside the waves are getting more and more impressive. The sea is truly ugly and beautiful at the same time, whitened by trails of foam.

During our brief night Gliksman has taken down all sail and put up a tiny storm jib. This little triangle, which measures 1.5 metres high by 3 metres wide, is enough to keep the boat heading into the waves, but it also means that we're making no progress, or very little. On the other hand, Gliksman seems more confident. He thinks we're entering the last stage of the depression. The air is colder, the wind is weakening and the waves are all over the place. According to him we're about to cross the cold front; the winds will still be violent and then in six hours at the most, the gale will be over. Besides, the Coast Guard weather station is still saying that the wind will drop to 20 knots. Later that morning he tries in vain, with Denis's help, to take an astronomical fix. The sun never comes out for more than thirty seconds and the swell makes it impossible to get an accurate reading. Feelings between father and son get heated during the quarter hour of this attempt. Denis is sitting on the after cabin top, his eye glued to the sextant eyepiece for five minutes, but without saying a word. His father, pencil poised over the chart table, gets impatient:

'This is stupid. Put the thing down. You'll never see anything.'

'Yes I will, wait. There's the sun... mark!'

Alain notes down the exact time, but ten seconds later he bursts out 'If you're going to wait ten minutes between your mark and your reading, you might as well go to bed!'

Denis gets cross, wipes the spray off the mirrors and starts again. This time he gives the degrees immediately after the mark, but as he makes Alain wait for the second series the latter throws down his pencil.

'No, no! You're too stubborn. You never do what you're told. It's not worth the trouble.'

A few hours later, Alain tries again. He takes the sextant and I take the pencil, but still no reading. Alain gives up. Pity, because I wanted to find out the secrets of celestial navigation. I'll have to wait for another time. At nightfall Alain suggests trying to raise Paris via Radio St-Lys, just for something to do. But when we open the chart table drawer, we have a nasty surprise: two of the four microphone leads have been pulled off. The radio must have been sliding around in all that pitching. We'll have to resolder the leads tomorrow morning. It'll give us a chance to try out the generator.

Olivier has improvised a sort of stew for dinner, made with eggs, sweetcorn and sausages. They all go off to eat it in the warmth of the stern cabin. But I prefer to stay at the helm. Seen from outside where the wind is icy and dollops of spray keep hitting me in the face, this dinner looks like a banquet. Inside, Gliksman is explaining for the Nth time his theories about changes in the weather in terms of the classic development of a depression. The cold front, which follows the squalls, is a line of violent disturbance. This line usually moves from southwest to northeast. We just have to let it pass peacefully by. About 3 a.m. the wind seems to fall. Denis and Olivier grab the chance to increase sail. They take in the storm jib and put the mainsail back up with three reefs; the staysail is half unrolled. *RTL-Timex* starts to make some headway again.

At daybreak on Saturday the sea looks the same, still as rough. We've been sailing for three nights and two days in this chaos and it doesn't impress us any more, but it is beginning to tire us out. Our chief thought now is to know if Olivier de Kersauson has left New York in *Kriter IV*: he's going to try to beat the Atlantic crossing record, like us. Since we have to have a competitor, it would be more exciting to leave at the same time as him. The two boats are roughly similar, only their age is different. They're both trimarans with first-class skippers, tested crews and two journalists on board. My three young crew mates can already see themselves at Deauville forming an arch of honour for the crew of *Kriter IV*. The point of this arch in terms of the race being none other than a fine salute from the victors to the vanquished: a form of salute that isn't quite an insult. We don't have long to wait. In one of their weather forecasts the Coast Guard announces that the Port of New York is closed due to bad weather. So Kersauson is trapped and has to wait for us. This announcement is greeted on board with loud laughter and applause for it means that the two teams can offer each other a gigantic blow-out in New York before confronting the frosts of the fiftieth parallel. The negative side of the Coast Guard's message isn't negligible, though Gliksman refrains from pointing it out. If the Port of New York is closed for the first time in its history, the depression we're in must be formidable. Personally I've nothing to compare it with, but what about the others?

Gliksman assures me that the sea was twice as rough at the start of the Route de Rhum race in the Gulf of Gascony. Alain Gouedard tells me of the two occasions when he had to sail with bare poles, in the English Channel and the Mediterranean. It's obvious that Denis has never sailed in such winds. Nor Olivier, but it doesn't seem to worry him at all. Dinner consists of 'special' pasta as conceived by Alain Gouedard, who is an excellent sailor but a poor cook. The mainsail has again to be rolled up on the boom. With the storm jib and 4 square metres of staysail, we're making between one and two knots. The fourth night will be an exact copy of the previous three. Gouedard hands me the helm at 6 a.m. – he's had enough of hanging about in the middle of the Atlantic: 'Great! We're making five or six knots: at this rate we'll arrive at New York on Wednesday evening.' For ten seconds, in the space between two waves, I see my first sharks, or rather their fins, 50 metres away from the starboard float and I can't help a slight shiver.

Unfortunately Gouedard spoke too soon and mid-morning we have to once again reduce what little sail we have to make headway with. From now on the sea shows its power. Several times I catch myself comparing the waves with the RTL building in the Rue Bayard in Paris. The needle of the wind-speed meter never dips below 45 knots; mostly it's at 50 but the occasional gust pushes it up to 60. All the wave crests are white while the troughs, swept by the wind, foam like the mouths of mad dogs. Great trails of foam show the strength of the wind. For Alain Gliksman they're more indicative than the anemometer: they mean force 10 or 11! For the first time since our departure I'm ill at ease. The boat is smashed about and I wonder if the floats, or their crossbeams, can take it. But apparently I'm the only one who's worried. The others are ecstatic before this Danté-esque spectacle. Gliksman has slipped into his oilskins and is giving a running commentary from the cockpit on the vastness of the waves, as if he were describing the colour of a rocket or a firework. 'Look at that monster – unbelievable! Oh and what about that one! Luckily it's going to miss us.'

The deafening crash as a wave breaks over the decks provokes swearing: 'The bastard! Watch out, here come its mates!'

The 'bastard and its mates' are three extra large waves which emerge at irregular intervals from the long Atlantic swell and get christened 'the three demons'.

At lunchtime Alain is discouraged by our protests from taking up a position at the stove: yesterday evening's experience was enough. Once again Olivier is chosen to cook us up something special from what ingredients we have left. Spaghetti does the honours again, enriched with an elaborate tomato sauce in such profusion that some is actually left over in the pan. About 4 p.m. Gliksman grumblingly notes down the latest Coast Guard weather forecast.

The night will not bring respite: winds of 70 knots are forecast. *RTL-Timex* is hitting harder and harder. Alain lets slip, 'Any minute now one of those waves is going to be wearing this boat like a hat.' With the helm down and a storm jib, our 16.30 metres aren't easy to handle. We must change tactics. The waves are getting too dangerous to tackle head-on: we must take them on the beam. At Gliksman's direction, Gouedard unrolls 2 square metres of staysail and returns to the helm to negotiate each wave. For the first quarter of an hour he seems tense, but gradually I can sense that he's enjoying it. 'Amazing! – I can make this boat's 16.30 metres work like the 5.20 of my Hobie cat at Deauville.'

Denis, well strapped down, tries for the second time to resolder the microphone leads. The previous night he'd got the green and the yellow wires mixed up. Olivier is sleeping happily, and as for me I'm taking kilometres of film. If I tell about my tempest at sea, no one will ever believe my stories of 12 metre waves. Even allowing for optical distortions, my film will supply indisputable proof. Denis has just finished his repairs. He too brings out his camera, then his cine camera, wrapped up in a plastic bag. I put my camera down on the forward cabin bunk, filled to the brim with 'shock' photos, and go to do fifty strokes at the pump. The float must be lightened under a wind that's packing in one breaker after another. Each float has two small access hatches of the Goiot type, which allow one to see at a glance the state of the interior of the floats, or in case of failure to introduce a bilge pump. Their plastic seals have no doubt lost their effectiveness, for the leeward float is diving under the waves most of the time and fills up slowly but surely.

Alain Gouedard will soon have been at the helm for two hours. Every five minutes a lump of seawater whips him across the face, blinding him for a few seconds. He seems very strained though he's still smiling. To make myself useful, I knot a sail tie round his waist to close up his oilskin as its zip has broken. Denis is still filming. Gliksman, seizing the chance of a trough, shoves his head out and advises Alain, 'Get Olivier to take over. You'll be clapped out and we still need your strength.' Five minutes later Alain and I pass on our orders and go into the after cabin. It's 6.30 p.m. He gets undressed, leaving on just his polar suit, an orange acrylic fur undergarment which covers him from ankles to neck. I take off just my oilskins and make some good hot tea. I can't explain why, but I have a bad feeling. Would I be better off going back into the cockpit with Olivier, or staying here with Alain and resting? Might as well get my strength back for the night: I'll try and sleep. For the first time I decide to go to bed as I am: with my tee-shirt, a roll-neck shirt, jeans, oilskin trousers and boots. I lie down and my gaze falls on the pan with its spaghetti leftovers. A brief image flashes through my mind of this pan flying into my face. I sit up and consider it for a moment and start asking myself the best way to wedge it so that it can't move. This is stupid, since it's been in the same place since we left. Why notice it today more than yesterday? I can't understand my disquiet faced with this utensil, and prefer to persuade myself that my worries are unjustified.

At 6.40 p.m. Gliksman changes his mind for the second time. Both the structure of the boat and the strength of the crew must be spared. The best solution is the storm jib. We'll throw out a sea anchor and wait for it to be over. Gliksman goes to get a rope and gives it to Denis who gets ready to go up on deck. As Gliksman tells it:

'At this moment I don't understand. The boat mounts a wave, heels incredibly, and instead of going over the crest, continues mounting. The starboard float gets caught, the water boils. Denis and I exchange a look of disbelief: "We can't be going over!" Jammed in the doorway, I don't even lose my balance. For a moment it seems as if the boat will steady herself, but then she rears up again to the vertical. Water pours into the cockpit all over Olivier while Denis seems to be scaling the bulkhead. He obviously doesn't know whether to jump into the water with Olivier or cling to a part of the steering gear. I cry out to them "Stay in the boat! Stay in the boat!" Denis is still hesitating. Everything on the chart table and its instruments fall on my head and I'm engulfed in water. The boat steadies herself at last – but she's been tossed over like a pancake! It's 7 p.m. The portholes, now under water, no longer admit the pale light of dusk. We're plunged into darkness. I immediately think of the survival capsule. The little hatch which closed it off fell off when we overturned. Its opening is just above my head. At this moment I'm convinced that Alain 2 and Nicolas have been drowned in the rear cabin.'

Denis is floating, trapped in the cockpit and crying out 'Olivier! Olivier! Make a noise, knock on the hull! In the after cabin, Alain and I are rolling about on top of one another, on the bunks, on the portholes and finally on the ceiling. All the kitchen implements are falling all over us. As if in a cartoon film, we see the saucepans rushing at us and the spaghetti pan lands on my head. Everything's confused. This nightmare, which in reality probably only lasted twenty seconds, seems to go on for a century. Alain was torn brutally out of his sleep and is completely stupefied. Very calmly I hear myself say 'O.K., so what happens next?'

Seated like me against the locker, on the ceiling become floor, he tries to get up, saying, 'The survival capsule....'

The water's rushing in through the shattered portholes, despite which I ask with the same surprising calm, 'And how do we get in?'

Rapidly pulling himself together, Alain has already slid his way two metres into the sort of black grotto under, or rather now over, the cockpit. I join him, hardly noticing that the water's up to my waist. The darkness of the capsule reminds me of the torch hung on a bracket on the bulkhead. It's gone. I glance round and plumb the water in a vain attempt to find it. Alain shouts 'Quick, the trapdoor!' He's already undone a dozen of the wing nuts which hold down the oval hatch to the open air. In barely thirty seconds they're all undone and we're frantically pulling on the handles to open it. Despite our efforts, the cover doesn't budge an inch. Denis is shouting from the other hatch (into the forward cabin) 'Olivier! Olivier! Knock on the hull!'

If Olivier is outside, we absolutely must get this stupid trapdoor open. We pull even harder and it gives. Without even thinking, Alain goes through into the forward cabin and asks Gliksman for the sledge-hammer. But the sledgehammer went to the bottom of the ocean at the same time as the generator and the tools when we overturned. Groping around at his feet, Gliksman finds a metal fitting instead. Alain goes into the cockpit and dives vertically as if leaving a submarine by the airlock. In trying to get to the outside, under water, he gets his feet caught up in some ropes and can't reach the surface. He finally manages it after a few mouthfuls of water. I'm alone again in the capsule: it seems to me all is lost. In these 12 metre high waves, Olivier must be drowned. We won't even find his body. I remember his unshaven face, his careless walk, and already I'm imagining how, if we're rescued, we're going to have to explain his disappearance. But with the night coming on and no end to the rough sea, I can't see how we're going to survive anyway. I hear Alain on the other side of the hull and his shouts cut short my despairing thoughts; 'Olivier is safe, Olivier is safe, he's over there!' He begins violently hitting the escape hatch. At the fifth blow the cover gives way and I see Alain's head outside framed in the opening.

'Pass me a rope. Olivier is on the rudder. We must get him in.'

Before doing this I can't stop myself shoving my head out and Olivier really *is* there, astride the overturned hull, grasping the rudder in his arms. Later he tells us: 'When I first found myself in the water, I swallowed a mouthful before getting back to the surface. It was a terrifying sight. There was an immense red stain round the boat. I though it was blood. I tried to find something to cling to, but there was nothing, nothing – no halyard, no sheet, nothing but the smooth hull. Two or three times I was swept away by waves and saw the boat moving away from me, but then the swell brought me back. I kept going under: I couldn't swim because of my boots so I had to get them off. Once I managed to grab the starboard runner, but a wave washed me off again, this time towards the stern and I knew I wouldn't be able to get back. Then, and really it was a miracle, as I was trying to get hold of the transom

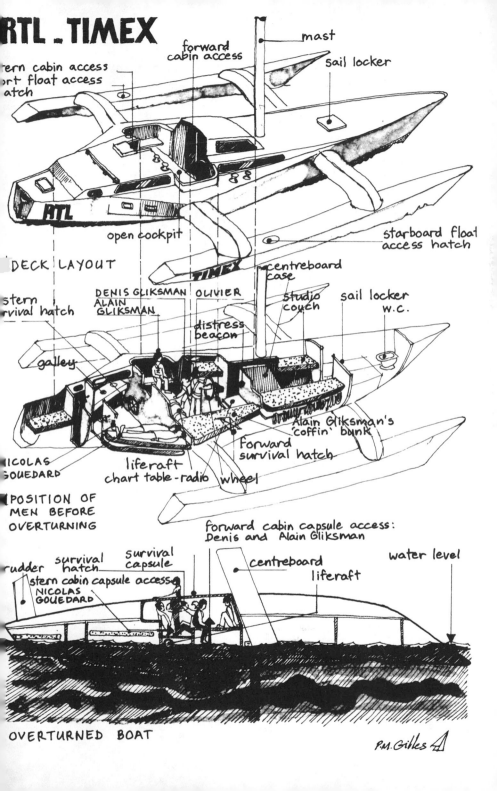

RTL . TIMEX

mast

forward cabin access

sail locker

stern cabin access
port float access hatch

open cockpit

starboard float access hatch

RTL

TIMEX

DECK LAYOUT

centreboard case

DENIS GLIKSMAN   OLIVIER

studio couch

sail locker
w.c.

stern survival hatch

ALAIN GLIKSMAN

distress beacon

galley

Alain Gliksman's 'coffin' bunk

NICOLAS GOUEDARD

liferaft
chart table-radio   wheel

Forward survival hatch

POSITION OF MEN BEFORE OVERTURNING

forward cabin capsule access:
Denis and Alain Gliksman

survival capsule

survival hatch

centreboard

water level

liferaft

rudder

stern cabin capsule access
NICOLAS GOUEDARD

OVERTURNED BOAT

P.M.Gilles

I felt the cable of the automatic pilot in my hands. I clung to it like a madman and managed to climb onto the rudder. I'd been there at least two minutes when Alain shouted to me. I thought you were all dead, trapped under the hull. I couldn't hear you and I was too out of breath to even try calling.'

We get Olivier back by throwing him a rope, the same rope which was about to be used for the sea anchor before we went over. Night has fallen. It hasn't yet dawned on us how lucky we all are to be safe. For the moment, we've got to rescue as much gear as possible, and above all, the liferaft. It's floating at the end of its line in the middle of the 'covered swimming pool' of the upturned cockpit.

Gliksman and Denis are still in the forward cabin, up to their chests in water, trying to push the raft container under the gunwale but the water pressure is too great. It'll have to be hauled from outside. As usual, Alain acts before speaking. Taking the rope he used to rescue Olivier, he dives through the trapdoor once more, shouting 'Wait, I'll do it from outside!' Once underneath the cockpit, he firmly lashes it to the container and all five of us coordinate our efforts. Alain (while swimming), Denis and his father (half submerged) try to push the 'bib' under the side of the cockpit. At the same time, Olivier and I try to pull the rope from above without losing it. The operation succeeds and the water pressure forces the white form of the container towards the outside. It's like one of those floats that you force beneath the surface in a swimming pool in order to make it leap in the air. For a moment we hesitate. Should we inflate it and get in immediately, or wait for the last possible moment? Gliksman thinks that the overturned *RTL-Timex* is more or less stable. Designed to be unsinkable, she'll make the best possible raft. While Denis and Alain rejoin Olivier and me,

Gliksman stays in the forward cabin, in a frenzy to save as much gear as possible. He hands everything he can find through the interior access hatch. The sextant, pilot books, box of flares, rolls of charts, dividers, more charts, a screwdriver, more charts. I don't understand the usefulness of half the stuff he's passing to me and I shout to him 'Clothes, try to find clothes – sleeping bags, blankets, oilskins!' Strangely, the radio has stayed on underneath the water for the past quarter of an hour, its little red light transforming the forward cabin into a luminous rectangle. The boat's still being thrown backwards and forwards and at each movement more gear washes out of the cabin.

Alain can't find anything else useful and climbs up to join us. It's a delicate arrangement; this miniature grotto was obviously not meant to accommodate five well-built men. We've got about 2.5 metres long by 1.5 wide by 80 centimetres at the highest point. Olivier squats in a corner saying nothing, trying to recuperate. Denis is wedged in the opening to stop the waves from getting in. Alain is beside him, his chin on his knees. Gliksman is resting his back against Alain's knees and I'm half lying on my side like a Roman, above the forward cabin trapdoor. Our position is so complicated that we still don't know whose foot is on whose shoulder, or whose leg against whose knee. It takes a good half hour to work out the best position. Somebody or other gets a cramp in the leg and everybody has to change position or double up even more. The only light we've managed to save comes from a little spare compass. It's hardly a glimmer since it was originally only intended to illuminate the needle and the figures, like a car dashboard light. Nevertheless this is the light that enables us to hunt around in the stern cabin and find a couple of onions, a jar of gherkins, a tin of chocolate powder, some Nescafé, two lemons, a bottle with a little syrup in the bottom and one of the bottles of wine taken on board at St George's. This was the wine that had drawn my attention to the survival capsule! Most important of all, two jerry cans of fresh water are hoisted up next to us, reducing our tiny space even more.

It's black night now and the general tendency is to doze. For a whole minute no one speaks. I feel like sleeping too, but Gliksman doesn't like this silence. 'Denis, are you all right?' 'Yes, yes.' 'What about you, Alain?' 'No problems.' 'Olivier? Olivier?' Olivier's already asleep, more exhausted than the rest and with good reason. Gliksman gets worried: 'Reply, come on, say something. We must keep awake.' Nobody really feels like talking. We're all thinking out our situation. We've capsized, we're all safe and sound, we're expected at New York, but will the boat hold together? Gradually these considerations fade into a kind of dream, with remorse, regrets, fear and hope, or in my case despair. But every ten to twenty minutes a freezing wave engulfs our little refuge with unbelievable force. The first few times the combined affect of the noise and cold of these breakers is frightful, freezing and soaking us ceaselessly. The sudden change of air pressure caused by the water forcing the air out blocks our ears like a plane at takeoff. Moreover, this fantastic surge of air, after the entry of a wave, tears out the sweaters and other things with which we've tried to plug the trap. We scream back curses at the violence of these waves, trying to replug the accursed opening.

During this first night we transmit several distress calls using the radio beacon. This enormous orange walkie-talkie transmits on 2182 kHz – any ship within a maximum of five miles which is tuned in to this maritime frequency should pick up our signals. But Gliksman doesn't kid himself; if a ship happens to be in the area there's very little chance that her radio operator will be awake listening for distress signals. We try four times, giving our estimated position as 36° north, 66° west, but the speaker remains silent all night. Our watches, which were provided by the boat's sponsors, are still working although they've clouded up, and the hours tick by with desperate slowness. About midnight Alain, who up to now hasn't complained, starts shivering. His polar suit underwear just isn't enough to protect him against the cold and above all the dollops of water which continually soak us. Gliksman, who's rescued two woollen pullovers, takes his oilskin jacket off and gives it to Alain. We're all ill-equipped. Denis may well have put on an anorak underneath his complete set of oilskins, but once wet, this garment never dries. His tracksuit is equally wet and will never warm up. With his shirt, two woollen sweaters, long-johns and oilskin trousers, Gliksman isn't suffering too badly from the cold but he also is permanently wet. It's the same for me. Although I managed to get hold of a sleeveless sweater and a quilted jacket, this latter is too long and drinks up water from the bottom of the boat like a wick. Alain Gouedard, who used to swim in the English Channel even in January, will be happy for a while with his long underwear and oilskins. As for Olivier, who says nothing, no one knows what he's got on under his oilskins. By the time we find out it'll be almost too late. When it's discovered that Alain and Olivier are barefoot a night fishing trip is organized in the stern cabin to unearth any pair of shoes or at the least some slippers. By a small miracle, Alain's pair of size 46 sports shoes, which he never wore, are found floating. But nothing, not even a pair of socks, can be found for Olivier.

So we pass the night, sweeping the water of the stern cabin, dozing, sending distress signals, but above all checking the water level in the hull. During the first two hours after capsizing the boat sank a few centimetres then steadied herself. Denis wakes up every half hour to gauge the rise of the water in the stern cabin. He doesn't disguise his concern and regularly suggests that we should get into the 'bib' without delay. The situation in the forward cabin is less worrying. I'm dangling my legs through the access trap, in order to make more room, and the distance between my feet and the water surface is an excellent indicator. From time to time Gliksman forces a discussion in an attempt to work out why we capsized. A mistake on Olivier's part is excluded for a start. A vicious gust of wind? It hardly seems likely with the tiny amount of canvas the boat was carrying. An analysis of the boat's movements leads us to the following provisional conclusion: the change from the warm to the cold front confused the wave pattern; waves were crossing and breaking more violently. A first wave, estimated at 12 metres, made the boat heel; her windward float caught the wind and before she could even begin to skid back, a second wave finished her off by lifting her bow.

Once this brief sketch of the capsize has been worked out, everyone sinks back into his own thoughts. Within a quarter of an hour I'm imagining the worst. Crammed in a corner of the survival capsule, I know that if the boat sinks suddenly I won't have time to get out. I end up hoping that it'll be quick, that I won't have time to realize what's 'happened'. Everything changes once one can imagine one's own death, once it seems near. At first one is surprised to find that one doesn't mind, then one objects. It's intolerable to think of disappearing without having the time to examine one's existence. On the other hand, one gets impatient and if it has to be ended wishes it could be over quickly. There's a strong desire to 'scream', but one mustn't give in to it because of the others. The basic theory is: 'if one breaks, the others will follow.'

There's always something that needs checking, repairing or changing, so we can't rest. Now the 'bib' is threatening to snap its mooring line. The ever-powerful waves carry it over to the other side of the hull with such wild force that it risks breaking. We double up on the line to be safe.

With the first dawn light we have to admit that the water has risen. Yesterday evening my feet were 20 centimetres from the water in the cabin; this morning they're up to the ankles and it's 6 a.m. Powerless, Gliksman has to admit that his so-called unsinkable boat is sinking slowly but surely. We ought to get ready to embark in the 'bib' but the sea's too dangerous for such an operation. We'll have to wait for the next calm. Looking beneath my feet, I can see that the mast has survived intact. I can see its form through the wheel-house windows, plunging into the unreal green depths of the ocean. My fear has disappeared with the return of the light, and I manage to admire the unusual sight of a mast turned into a keel. Which doesn't prevent me from observing the first-aid kit, floating a metre from my right foot. The instant it's near enough, I grab it and put it on my lap. It's a real magic chest and I take out everything that could possibly have a use, even non-pharmaceutical. Adhesive bandage, safety-pins, an aluminium sheet for burn cases, scalpel blades, surgical spirit, a wound disinfectant capsule, and a rubber tourniquet. I feel like Robinson Crusoe sorting through these treasures.

Depending on the angle of the hull, little rays of sunlight touch our faces like caresses. It's all we needed to get our courage back. After all, if we're all alive after the capsize, and we've got through the first night O.K., there's no reason why things should get worse now.

We're not the first to founder in the history of ocean racing. Obviously we'll be picked up within twenty-four hours at the most, like the others.

3

'Lost at Sea'

T he float's sunk a lot deeper since yesterday
evening. She won't hold out much longer.'

Denis seems really very worried. All night he's been
observing the water level in the stern cabin; it has risen
perceptibly. When we first settled in on the survival
platform the level was steady at a metre lower. Now the
water's just touching the floor and, depending on the
angle, tiny ripples are licking the floor of our quarters.
The starboard float isn't playing its supporting role
very well in this instance, yet the designer had boasted
about the boat's buoyancy in a capsize, precisely
because of the floats. Far more of the hull is under water
than yesterday and she hardly reacts any more to the
undiminished onslaught of the waves. But the swell has
lengthened, reducing the effects of the troughs. Since we
really must abandon the wreckage if we don't want to
be drowned like rats, we must take advantage of this
relative calm. Denis, his body three-quarters outside, is
explicit: 'We're sinking by the stern. We must be quick
– she won't last two hours.'

Once again it's Alain 2 who takes charge of the
operation with Gliksman advising. He climbs out along

the crossbeam and ties a rope to the cord which goes into the 'bib' container. By pulling hard we should get it opened and inflated. The instructions on the case indicate that one should: first anchor the retaining rope to a strong point on the deck; then throw the raft into the sea. And it will open automatically! But what the manufacturer hadn't thought of, and we discover, is that an overturned hull doesn't offer a strong fixing point. Moreover, there's a big difference between these two operations: throwing a raft down from a height of 1.5 metres or pushing it out away from the hull of a floating wreck. The first time Alain tries pulling on the cord alone; the raft bobs about like a cork but doesn't respond. The second attempt is equally fruitless. So he gets back into the capsule. Denis helps him prepare another try and Gliksman mutters 'That's all we needed, for it not to open!'

It's something I hadn't thought of. Olivier's blank expression reveals his thoughts, that are the same as mine: 'We couldn't be that unlucky. It will open. It will open. It must open. Otherwise we're hopelessly lost.'

Alain's cry of victory is a relief. 'O.K., the case is off, it's unfolding. Shit! It's upside down... no, it's all right, it's turning over. Wonderful, it's inflated!

There isn't a minute to be lost. The agony of the past few hours is expelled by the activity of this new embarkation. Denis jumps first, after checking the doubled line, followed by Olivier, then Gliksman. We have to slide along the hull, hanging onto the edge of the escape hatch like monkeys. Crouching on the narrow edge of the platform, our arms extended, we have to somehow turn round and throw ourselves through the opening of the raft's canopy. Although the swell is longer the waves are still as high. The 'bib' goes up and down and we end our jumps half in the water, half draped over the rubber tube. Left alone in the capsule, I pass them all the gear we recovered during the night: the box of flares, the two jerry cans of fresh water, then I think for a moment. Is it really worth carrying all this fresh water for a few hours in a liferaft? It's going to weigh us down and get in the way. Besides, I'm not even thirsty. My action has preceded my thought, the 40 litres of water are in the raft before I've got to the end of this piece of reasoning. Gliksman shouts to his son 'Lash them down with whatever you can find, right now!'

I hadn't noticed it till now, but outside the noise of the wind and the waves drowns our voices; you have to scream to make yourself heard.

'The compass and the sextant!' Gliksman is still obsessed with rescuing his navigation instruments. 'The Pilot, find the Pilot!' I wonder what use this book will be to us either. But I obey orders like an automaton. It looks more like a paving-stone from the Quartier Latin than a nautical book. It's soaked, the cardboard cover sticks to my fingers, and its few hundred pages form a solid lump. I chuck it to Gliksman like a rugby ball. I decant the first-aid kit into a plastic bag and throw it into the 'bib', but with more care than I used with the book. As soon as the survival platform is clear, I gather up lemons here and onions there and other provisions saved from drowning.

I dispatch two anoraks and a duvet, which end up in the water because of the wind. Luckily they're immediately recovered.

'Look alive.' Alain 2 is still standing on the hull waiting for us to finish before casting off. At the exact moment when I let go of the edge of the hatch and jump into the 'bib', I catch sight of Alain's shoes, which he hadn't managed to put on during the night because of the lack of space. As I cling to the rubber float, I shout to him 'Your shoes are still inside.' I hope he's heard as I'm grabbed by Olivier and Gliksman and our new craft is set rocking.

Our evacuation isn't complete in that we're prisoners: the 'bib' is trapped to its right and left by the hull and the float, fore and aft by the crossbeams. Depending on the waves, our rubber craft hits one or other of these four barriers. Alain tries to haul the 'bib' over the forward crossbeam by hoisting himself up lengthwise on the hull, but we're too heavy. We must reduce the weight by getting out again. Olivier gets up on the hull with Alain. Denis and I flounder about half clinging to the float and half to the raft, trying not to lose our waterlogged boots and not to sink like stones for our oilskin trousers are also full of water. As Gliksman prepares to join us in the drink, the raft is already on the crossbeam and sliding over to the other side. Strangely enough, the water isn't particularly cold at 8 o'clock on this Sunday morning. Frozen by cold and fatigue, I find it almost warm. At our insistence Olivier finally joins us in the water, while Alain disentangles the mooring line which has got all knotted up due to the disordered movements of the 'bib'. This craft is exactly how I imagined it; two big black rubber tubes form a hexagon crowned with a third tube which serves as an arch. It's covered with an orange canvas tent-like canopy, dotted with small reflecting strips and glued to the arch and three of the six sides of the raft. It's held closed only by small elastic loops and toggles like those on a duffle coat. Within ten minutes of embarking, we've realized how extremely weakly designed the 'bib' is. In fact we're losing one of the elastic toggles which join the flaps. I see this new phase of our rescue like an astronaut waiting to be picked up after a trip in space. The overturned *RTL-Timex* looks more like a UFO than a racing yacht, and our 'bib' has the same shape as the rafts we saw on television during the last recovery stages of the Apollo missions. I can practically hear the sound of the rescue helicopters; my imagination takes off and all I need is the distant silhouette of an aircraft carrier to complete the picture. Alain, still standing on the ridge of the blue hull, adds to the image. He looks like a NASA technician in his orange polar suit and yellow oilskins. His situation is becoming dangerous: if he doesn't jump at once he'll have to swim, and to swim near the wreck in this chaos would be too risky. There's a metre and a half between the two craft and Alain leaps it in a magnificent bound. His arrival in the 'bib' is greeted with howls of pain from Gliksman and his son for it's their legs that soften the fall of his 70 kilos. Denis is hanging on firmly to the line which links us to the wreck. This 50 metre 'umbilical cord' quickly doubles the distance between us and the 'mother' ship. The tension is too great and the line cuts into his hands. The 'bib' is lighter than the trimaran and drifts ahead of her. It's as if we were towing a truck with a bicycle, going up the hills faster, but then being caught up going down. Thus, when we're in a trough the trimaran begins to slide and 'planes' at us like a battering ram. Denis cries out in terror 'It's stupid! She's charging us! She's going to bloody capsize us! We must let go!'

Gliksman bursts out 'No, hang on! The overturned hull is a good bit easier to spot than this speck of rubber.' But when he sticks his head outside the tent and sees this enormous surfboard hurling itself at us, he orders 'Let go! Let go!' then adds, sadly, 'Too bad. But if we want to stay in one piece....' All the same, I'm finding it difficult to realize just how serious our position is, and judging by the attitudes of my companions in misfortune I'm not the only one. I don't know if it's the excitement, fatigue or relief, but we're all cracking jokes, albeit with an effort.

'Big ground-floor, eh?'

'I hope someone's brought the playing cards.'

'I should've brought my chess set.'

'Good God, if Kersauson could see us.'

Or even: 'We'll have to do better than this to beat the record.'

Alain, who right to the end will manifest a sometimes exasperating optimism, adds: 'What a pity we'll be taking a shower on a ship by tonight, and won't even have the chance to enjoy it.'

Meanwhile these sallies don't prevent us from bailing out the water that came on board during our evacuation. The 'bib' has become a kiddies' paddling pool. Olivier, Denis and I are wildly refilling the three mugs saved from the wreck. Gliksman starts to do an inventory of the raft's equipment and finds a butterfly net, a sort of little parachute made of mosquito netting and attached to a tiny orange cord the size of a telephone lead. 'I don't believe it – it can't be the sea anchor. It's a toy!' He can't accept that this device will hold us in the right position in relation to the waves. For the want of anything better, it's dumped in the drink. It takes up its position in thirty seconds and the first blow to slew the raft round proves that it does its job well enough. Inside, we're all more or less doubled up. Denis and I on the wave side, Alain and Olivier opposite, Gliksman in the middle. We still can't sit. The rescued gear and the survival kit are littered about the bottom of the 'bib' and are still submerged in water. It's already ten minutes since we left the wreck and the muddle all round us is hardly favourable for taking stock of our position.

At about 9 p.m. a hedge-hopping jet plane comes straight for us making an appalling din. I'm struck on the back with such violence that I'm thrown across the raft. Olivier and Alain are sucked up into a soaring flight and fall into the sea three metres away. The raft overturns and throws Denis and me out into the foaming middle of a roller that's just exploded over our heads. I'm half knocked out: I can't remember where I am. The water's warm. My muscles have been tense since the evening before and begin to relax. It's so good just to let go! It would be a dream to stop moving, stop thinking, give up completely. For what seems like an eternity, I allow myself to be overcome by this sense of well-being, not even trying to understand what has happened. I'm not drowning in the middle of the Atlantic, I'm floating somewhere. It isn't water supporting me anymore, it's . . . nothing, nothingness, weightlessness. I don't know, but it feels good. I want it to continue. I no longer need to speak, to move. My body has lost its weight. It's suspended. I'm rocked gently, in a cradle perhaps. Besides I feel sleepy and I'm going to sleep. It's even nicer when I close my eyes. All these sensations come with such mildness. I can't concentrate on anything. My head feels light and empty. I don't even try to hold onto an image. My mind is completely liberated. I savour the moment; I even have the impression of giving little sighs of satisfaction.

'Nicolas, where's Nicolas?' Gliksman's call makes me open my eyes. To get my bearings I grab an anorak which is floating just by my right hand. Alain, who's spotted me, reassures the others: 'It's all right, he's over there.' And there I am, in fact, three metres from the 'bib'. Gliksman, Olivier and Alain are back inside. Denis is the only one still splashing about, hanging on to a trailing line, trying desperately to capture the sextant with his free hand as it floats gradually further and further away in its beautiful varnished box. Bad-temperedly, Gliksman almost snarls: 'Let the bloody thing go, I don't need it. Get back in, quick.' Gliksman's lying when he says he 'doesn't need it': he's had the same one for ten years. He used it to do his two solo Atlantic crossings, it's been round the world, round the Horn, across the Pacific. It's not just a navigational instrument anymore, it's like an old friend. Gliksman had hoped to give this 'old friend' a gentler end, an honourable retirement on the mantlepiece of his house at Flexanville. Now I know why it was the first thing he handed out last night from the cabin into the survival capsule. Gliksman's sextant will have a traditional seaman's dignified death: 'lost at sea'.

It's only now, a month later, that I realize the full drama of this scene: a father sees his son near to drowning before his very eyes. And the son is taking this risk to save a sextant, a miserable sextant. At the time, Olivier, Alain and I had no idea of this equation. We were five shipwrecked sailors, sharing the same responsibility, giving equal value to one another's lives, perhaps more than to our own. The only possible barrier which might come up is age. On the one hand four kids, on the other Gliksman, forty-six years old. Until this first day in the 'bib' a few reprimands to his son have been the only reminder of their family tie. This was certainly a conscious decision to prevent problems of jealousy between individuals, and there haven't been any. Denis has followed his father and played the game. On the trimaran he wasn't the skipper's son, but a member of the crew like everyone else. If anything, Gliksman tended to be more demanding towards him than towards us. An unpleasant position to be in, as I know only too well, from the same experience crewing for my father on the Vauriens and 420s of my childhood.

With the anorak between my teeth I swim back to the raft, trying to recover a duvet on the way. It's floating just below the surface, but having got hold of it I find I can't tow it. It's soaked through like a sponge and weighs too much, so regretfully I have to leave it behind or risk not making it back to the raft myself. Back at the rubber tube, I take the time to remove my waterlogged boots and hand them with the anorak up to Alain. As I'm about to get back in I change my mind as I badly need to pay heed to a call of nature. I explain what I'm doing to Alain, who's giving me a funny look: 'Oh, I see.' During this operation I remember that divers often use this technique to warm themselves up, and actually it's not a bad idea. Getting back into the 'bib' is easier because it's sitting lower in the water, for the very good reason that there's as much water inside as outside. Although rapidly righted by Olivier and Alain, who had buttressed it by pulling on the handles provided for the purpose, the 'bib' has taken on the maximum amount of water. On the other hand, disaster is all around it. Half the gear saved from the shipwreck has gone overboard. Jars of gherkins and Nescafé disappear and reappear like corks at the crest of waves. The gutted packet of chocolate powder leaves a little dark patch. A lemon sails, an onion sinks following the same route as the bottle of wine. We just manage to save the bag in which Alain had rescued some papers. The Pilot book has gone, along with a large tin of fat discovered at the last moment by Alain. The two jerry cans of fresh water and the box of flares are hanging outside at the end of their moorings, luckily made two minutes before overturning, with strips of bandage. The three mugs, which we hadn't yet had the time to tie down, have miraculously remained on board and are already back in use as bailers.

This first experience shows us the chief danger in this liferaft. And the noise of the wave which overturned us, like a jet passing the sound barrier, is engraved in our memories. We're going to hear this noise every five or six minutes for eight days and eight nights and each time our stomachs will turn over. It's real physical fear which knots the bowels, freezes the limbs and whitens the face. At the moment, the gap isn't very long. About four or five seconds pass between the moment the wave begins to break with an appalling din and the moment when it strikes the raft. It isn't the fear of being thrown into the water and dying that consciously worries us. It's quite simply terror of 'the wave', or more exactly, the noise of the wave. I suppose this must be the same phenomenon as that produced by the paralysing shout used in karate. One can't analyse this fear, it's simply a physical reaction, which disappears as soon as it comes. One tries to forget it immediately and practically gets used to it with repetition. If one of us were alone on this raft, perhaps he'd suffer it without trying to reduce its effects. But with five of us we feel it more strongly, both physically and morally. It gives us the will to fight. The only way to avoid another capsize is for all of us to take up a position on the side towards the wave, regardless of the effects of this on our comfort. Four of us sit with our backs pressed against the tube, the fifth is on his knees, his head shoved outside to warn of the arrival of dangerous waves. As soon as the lookout sees a breaker forming, he shouts 'wave coming!' Like motorcycle sidecar riders, we push as hard as we can on the float and the lookout flings himself on top of us. Our 300 kilos swung against the impact point of the wave prevent the raft from lifting. This is a trying business, but it's effective. Since the sea shows no signs of calming we have to renew this operation every ten minutes of this first day.

The second source of fatigue comes straight after the first. If we manage to prevent another capsize, we never manage to prevent water from getting into our little home. It gets in through the openings in the tent. There's only a five-centimetre overlap and the force of the wind and the mass of water falling all over the tent force the flaps apart. Thus the very instant after the confrontation with the breaking wave, we're treated to a magisterial cold shower which soaks us to the bones before refilling the raft. We try to keep the bottom dry by systematically bailing out and sponging, but before we can finish a new shower arrives and we have to start all over again.

We've been in the 'bib' three-quarters of an hour and, with this problem sorted out, it becomes urgent to check through the survival equipment. As well as the clothes we're wearing, there are two anoraks (you might as well say two sponges) and the thin aluminium sheet found in the first-aid kit. An onion and a half-squashed lemon are all that's left of the provisions we embarked with. The liferaft survival kit consists of: three bags, each containing a kilo of glucose tablets and vitamin biscuits. With the ten tins of 0.9 litre supplied with the raft and our two jerry cans of 20 litres, we're not short of drinking water. The remains of some sugar syrup complete the list. The manufacturer of the 'bib' has provided the following for everyday use: two sponges, a measuring jug, a very short fishing line, two fish hooks, a flexible canvas bucket, first-aid kit, a torch and two spare batteries. For safety and rescue there are: a signalling mirror, two rocket flares with parachutes, six hand flares, a float repair kit and two patches. Because of the way this equipment is installed in the bottom of the raft, we can't do a complete inventory the first day. It's all held together in a big compartmentalized plastic bag, but we fear that the instant we open it a wave will overturn us. At first glance, everything seems to us to be too small. The bailer is the shape and size of a baby's bottle. The fishing line wouldn't hold out against a struggling sardine. The fishhooks couldn't catch a mackerel in the Channel. The first-aid kit wouldn't please a kiddie who wanted to play at 'doctors'. It contains a tube of ointment for sprains, another for burns or infections, a pair of round-tipped scissors, a tiny strip of gauze, and some sea-sickness pills. The floating knife, stowed on the float, can barely cut an anorak cord. A salesgirl in a department store could just about wrap up a present with the two bits of 'string' which moor the sea anchor and the grabrope which is supposed to help recover a man overboard. As for the torch, which obviously ought to be waterproof, it's already mouldy and quite useless.

On this particular Tuesday morning it makes us laugh: it's too much. Someone must have wanted to play a joke on us. But later it will plunge us into silent rage, each time we realize that we can't fish, signal our position, or secure our safety. It's twenty-four hours since we last ate anything and even though we're not hungry Gliksman persuades us to have two vitamin biscuits each to get our strength back. These have got all mixed up with the glucose tablets in the bags and their distribution is somewhat chancy. In the absence of any directions, we can't yet tell the difference between these two sorts of 'shortbreads': one is white and strong, the other beige and crumbly. Gliksman doesn't feel at all well after eating his first tablet, which he describes as sweet and sickly, whereas we've been eating a tasteless paste. We become obsessed with the variety of our meals; the vitamin biscuit (beige tablet) for starters, the glucose (white tablet) as dessert. It's not that they're actually bad, but it's difficult to assert that these biscuits of 5 centimetres long by 3 wide by 0.7 thick have any particular taste. We have to chew them, or pretend to chew them, for a long time for them to be effective and to give the illusion of a meal. As they're certainly very rich in protein and calories, we mustn't eat them too rapidly, or they'll be difficult to digest. At least we're certain not to overeat. This first banquet is washed down with water from the tins. The two little tin-openers are put away immediately after use in the pockets of Alain's and Olivier's oilskins, which leads me to say 'Don't both go out at once, or we won't be able to drink.'

Such facetiousness might seem out of place under the circumstances. However, it gets used often afterwards. In fact, this facile humour is certainly an unconscious reaction to our situation which helps us to keep our spirits up and forcefully ignore our hostile environment. A good laugh cures all ills. This saying will be confirmed many times; it's also a form of discretion, allowing us to hide our distress. Choosing to behave like this tends to prove that we're holding out and keeping our spirits up, with no other explanation needed, and is one of our luxuries, like sleeping, or keeping more or less dry. No books, no films, no cards, no good meals, no fire in the grate, none of those little pleasures that improved life on land though we didn't notice at the time. So why deprive oneself of the luxury of a laugh on a bit of rubber in the middle of the Atlantic?

The water from this first tin is particularly foul, having taken on the taste of the tin it's been in for a year. Later our taste buds will be less demanding, but this first day they can still tell the difference between spring water and this tinned stuff, so that we empty the tin and chuck it overboard. 'Perhaps someone will find it and come looking for us.' For a moment this hope touches my mind, which is finally beginning to think like a castaway. But this stupid thought doesn't stay afloat for long before sinking without trace. Alain has been the first to play the role of lookout, judging perfectly the size, force, amplitude and frequency of the waves, thereby enabling us to avoid counterbalancing unnecessarily or too late. He asks to be replaced because he's exhausted and can't see anything any more. One must

look, over as wide an angle of vision as possible, simultaneously 2 metres away, 10 metres away, and at the
horizon: 2 metres away for the nearest wave, 10 metres
away for the following one, and everywhere else for a
possible ship. I offer to replace him, if only for a change
of position. In fact every move is like a Chinese puzzle in
a craft that measures a metre and a half in diameter. If
anyone shifts in this tiny space where we're balanced
precariously, the other four must quickly compensate.

It takes a good five minutes to get used to the
violence of the scene and its sonorous accompaniment.
The ocean is still as angry. It's still foaming and the
troughs are still unreasonably deep. For the first half
hour I'm not good at guessing the distance between the
raft and the breakers, because I've never done such a
thing before. I either over- or under-estimate the
moment when the wave is going to break, and conse-
quently the moment when it's going to strike us, or
simply harmlessly lift us up. The other four are subjected to a series of pointless and belated balancing
exercises. They only swear when they get doused with
icy water. I'm on my knees in the bottom of the raft and
for ten minutes I've been feeling taps through the
rubber, as if my legs were being pecked at. I keep
moving a few centimetres, but the irritation continues,
not really painful, but very annoying. We've got company. A small yellow fish and four silver, yellow and
blue ones, roughly 60 centimetres long, are swimming
round the raft and trying to bite the rubber where it's
pushed out by our bodies. Later, Olivier identifies our
new companions. They're dorado, also known as gilt-
headed bream, lively fish with sharp teeth. They're not
dangerous for us, but are so voracious that they fling
themselves at anything that approaches them. At least
Olivier asserts that this is so, because he's caught them

in the past. While I undertake my turn as lookout as seriously as possible, the others start to try and rearrange the inside of the raft to improve our comfort. When he unties one of the jerry cans Denis discovers a third air pump. The first two are for pumping up the flotation tubes and the tent arch, but we hadn't realized, this third one is for pumping up the bottom, the only part not to be inflated automatically with CO_2. Once filled, the bottom is like a ridged air-mattress with an exaggerated shape. It's not that much more comfortable than before, but it has the advantage of isolating us from the cold and the vicious attacks of our travelling companions. On the other hand, our ever-present paddling-pool is now diverted into an irrigation channel which runs right round the raft. From now on there'll be a more or less permanent 5 to 10 centimetre deep stream of water right where we're sitting against the tubes. As things get put away, we have to exercise our imaginations to find new ways of tying down everything that's left. Bandage from the first-aid kit is rinsed to remove the adhesive and used to strengthen the jerry can lashings. Anorak hood cords are used to tie down bailers. A strip of adhesive plaster fixes the distress beacon's aerial along the tent arch. Everything that can't be directly tied down is put in a canvas bag and hung on the cord handholds round the circumference of the floats. Another sad discovery interrupts this tidying-up session: the distress radio beacon's aerial has disappeared during the capsize. Gliksman and Gouedard cut off three-quarters of the long woven steel lead which serves as a ground aerial and let it hang in the water. With a lot of trouble, they manage to fix the rest in place of the vanished aerial and run it up to the top of the canopy, greatly reinforced with anorak cords. This repair is followed by an immediate test. Alain pushes the button that starts the automatic signal: it emits a sort of unstable modulated note, reminiscent of American police cars. Alain calls in bad English:

'Mayday, Mayday, Mayday. *RTL-Timex. RTL-Timex.* We are on a raft. We are on a raft. Our last position was thirty-six degrees north, sixty-six west. I repeat...'

Alain tries this three times with Gliksman correcting him: 'Slower. Separate your words.' After a minute's silence with his ear glued desperately to the silent loudspeaker, Alain cuts the transmission hoping for better luck next time.

We haven't finished with unpleasant discoveries. The water that is pouring round the gutter of the 'bib' uncovers safety pins and scalpel blades here and there, as if at low tide. Luckily, the safety pins haven't come open and the blades are lying flat. Without even thinking about it, and in a retrospective cold sweat, we chuck all this stuff overboard and organize a hunt for any other sharp, cutting or pointed objects. Everyone carefully slides a hand underneath this bottom to root out any possible 'weapon' that could put a quick stop to life on board our raft.

Denis has just replaced me at the lookout post. He's appalled at the sight he discovers and considers each wave to be the 'final' one. In ordering us 'all forward' he adds 'We've had it this time!' The tension mounts and I'm amazed that our muscles still respond to our wills.

For four hours now we've been counterbalancing one side or the other; we've been bailing out, sponging, arranging things, sponging, again and again. There hasn't been a moment's respite since we embarked, yet we're still holding out, and we will hold out as long as we have to. If we were to stop, we'd capsize again and it isn't sure that everyone would make it back on board.

Gliksman's about to put forward the catch-phrase,

the *sine qua non* condition: 'We must stick it out.' Stick it out, because others who've been shipwrecked have proved that survival depends on willpower. Gliksman keeps repeating his phrase. 'we must stick it out', as if to convince himself of it, until it's imprinted in our brains in indelible ink. The shipwreck of the Robertson family comes to mind, showing the sound foundation of this philosophy. They were adrift for nearly forty days a few years ago, and we've all read the story of their odyssey or at least heard about it. The forty days that they were adrift both terrifies and reassures us. Forty days is a long time, but if a family with children, a woman and a foreigner could survive that long, there's absolutely no reason why the five of us, all friends albeit not for long, and in good health, shouldn't endure it as well. Confronted with our doubts about the possibility of holding on for forty days in a stormy sea, Gliksman finishes his reasoning with reference to his own statistics: most castaways are rescued within three days of their boats being lost. In all the years he's been sailing, he's always encountered ships in every ocean of the world. We're about 300 kilometres from Bermuda and 600 from America so why shouldn't we encounter one of these ships?

My natural pessimism is about to get the upper hand, demolishing his argument. I regret my reply from the first word, but it's too late, I've got to finish my sentence: 'Your statistics make no mention of those who never came back to tell the story.'This uncalled-for remark puts paid to Gliksman's attempt to get our spirits up and he's completely confused. I perceive the discomfort I've caused with this thought, which Olivier expresses by pretending to be asleep, Alain by asking Denis a question, and Gliksman by some dedicated sponging in the bottom of the raft. I'm angry with myself for speaking so fast. I know that one must avoid this kind of defeatist talk at all cost; it's exactly the kind of thinking that destroys the will to survive. I'm going to have to control this weak point in my behaviour. I realize that whereas elsewhere this tendency to pessimism only has ill-fated consequences for me, in this enclosed space it contaminates four people. For even the ever-optimistic Alain has been cast down by my counterattack. It seems that defeatism can be infectious in the same way as fear. I won't forget this lesson: I must hide everything that might have an ill effect on the morale of the group.

Gliksman is anxious to know where the wind and waves are taking us and takes a bearing with the spare compass, recovered the previous evening *in extremis*. The needle wavers between 0° and 020°, or NNE. This couldn't be called the best route; it's carrying us away from both Bermuda and the United States, but on the other hand it may be carrying us into the shipping lanes between the European or African coasts and New York. This also means that the wind's from the south, and in the words of the old proverb '*Suroit le doux, quand il fache devient fou*', or in other words, a southwesterly is always bad news because when it gets angry there is a tempest.

Gliksman warns us, 'Save your strength. We're in for another battering tonight.' Then, as if to convince himself that he isn't mistaken, he parts the flaps and looks casually into the distance. Suddenly, he's on his knees: 'Wait, I thought I saw something... Olivier, look there, can you see anything?' And in fact, as soon as the raft is on top of a wave, Olivier confirms it: 'I think it's a ship!' I want to shout 'You *think*, or you're sure?' My heart's beating so hard that my temples are throbbing. I hold my breath. I can't stand it and, ignoring the laws of equilibrium, I get my head out. I see her at the same time as them. There she is, right on the horizon. It's late afternoon and the low sun makes her hull practically glow like a mirage. Alain is already rummaging in the box of flares. He gets a parachute type out, slowly it seems to me. His clumsy movements coupled with our own rock the raft dangerously. I decide to give up the amazing sight of the ship's silhouette on the horizon in order to help him launch the flare in the best conditions. I grip his legs between mine and hang on to his oilskins. The detonation is followed by the whistle of the rocket's climb into the air. Gliksman reacts: 'No, not a flare, it's useless in daylight. Anyway he's too far away. No point in deluding ourselves.' During the thirty seconds of the flare's descent our eyes are sometimes on it, and sometimes on the ship. The red flame has hardly died behind a wave when Gliksman breaks the seal on the big smoke bomb and throws it into the water as if it were a real bomb. It lights and thick grey smoke pours out for about a minute. But instead of rising into the air it flows over the water's surface, beaten down by the violent wind. 'The beacon, the beacon! He can't see us, perhaps he'll hear us!' Gliksman hasn't noticed Alain pulling on the cord of another flare, an ordinary one this time. 'No, no more flares. I told you it's useless. In any case he's too far away,' he says again, adding 'We must keep them for the night.'

I've let go of Alain's oilskins to busy myself with the radio beacon. In English as crude as his, I transmit 'Mayday, Mayday. We are on a raft. We can see you. We are on your left. Mayday. Mayday.'

Perhaps I don't sound convincing enough. Denis tears the beacon out of my hands and tries again, while all that's left is a tiny black point disappearing in the distance. Nothing. We can't make out anything at all in the crackling from the loudspeaker. Everyone tries to hide their disappointment. We find it difficult to swallow. Our throats are tight, but we try to hide it, our reaction limited to a shrug of the shoulders, underlined with a disillusioned smile. To make amends for my earlier mistake, I also put forward a new theory: as far back as one can go, no castaway has ever been rescued by the first boat encountered. The most likely average would be to be saved by the third. In fact there's no point in worrying until after this third ship. In the meantime we must expect to encounter other ships that won't even detect our presence. Gliksman vouches for my theory, explaining that nowadays, with automatic pilots, it's quite rare for an officer to be on the bridge. But in practice, even if there is a watch on the bridge the duty officer doesn't spend his time looking at the water. There's not even much chance that he'll notice a flare to port or starboard. Gliksman is emphatic: the best chance of being picked up is at night when a ship has the raft directly in its path. Even then, the duty officer might be below having a coffee, or in the case of a Liberian vessel sleeping peacefully in his bunk! Alain Gouedard, who doesn't seem to have heard Gliksman, exlaims with a big smile, 'There'll be a ship tomorrow. That way we'll have a good story to tell our mates. Just one day would sound pretty shabby.' Gliksman, not in the least surprised at Alain's spirit, continues: 'This boat proves that we're on a shipping route. There'll be others. We must be on the lookout.'

It's Olivier's watch. His 'Watch out! Here comes one!' is followed by the inevitable cold shower and raft refilling. The task of bailing and sponging begins again. We form a chain, some bailing, some pouring overboard. The technique still needs perfecting. The jerry cans are in the way and the compass is sticking in Alain's back. Without noticing, I've sat down on the beacon which we haven't had time to tie down again. As the night's coming on, we try to rearrange our small space intelligently, using the jerry cans as valuable stools, which insulate us from the wet bottom, and the flare box as a briefcase. The rest of our gear is hung on the inside grabropes opposite. This new tidying session uncovers the lemon and the onion. They're completely squashed and certainly got trampled on during the appearance of the ship. Against my advice and to my great despair, they're fed to the fish. Gliksman decides to hand out two new tablets before it starts getting cold again. When he opens the plastic bag, he finds disaster: half the opened packet has become a foul mess. The vitamin tablets, wrapped in twos in greaseproof paper, have not only been trampled on, but also doused with seawater. We manage to eat them by sucking them up and licking them from our hands. We drink a bumper mouthful of fresh water each from the jerry cans to get rid of the salty taste (the tinned water doesn't attract us any more). From now on the canvas bag will be hung from the top of the arch to keep it out of the semi-permanent puddle in the bottom.

The raft is equipped for the night with two tiny lights glued to the centre of the arch, one inside for our use, one outside for rescue purposes. The latter never lights, despite all our efforts. Their power is from two accumulators which can be recharged with seawater. You just have to fill them up to get two to three hours of power. So we prepare to spend our first night on board this contraption beneath this feeble light. While one person acts as lookout, the other four can sleep. Alain offers to take the first watch and we don't decide the others in advance. When he's tired, he'll wake up someone else and so on. The most important thing is that someone should always be on the lookout for a ship in our vicinity. As Gliksman explained that afternoon, we're twice as likely to be picked up at night. There's no question of lying down. The best we can do is stretch out our legs, criss-crossing them with our neighbour's. If someone gets cramp, untangling them is liable to be painful. It's best to sleep curled up, for one thing for the comfort of others and for another because you lose less heat in this position. Getting our legs, arms, behinds and heads into the right position takes half an hour. Alain unfolds the aluminium sheet and throws it over our legs as he's the only one who can move his arms without undoing this human knot. My head's resting on Olivier's shoulder. I close my eyes... sleep at last... the noise of a jet plane then a blow, a cold shower. Perhaps I'll be able to sleep later.

4

Punishment

They're magnificent! Two three-masted schooners have been racing for five minutes under full sail. One follows the other, overtakes, sometimes melts into it. The whiteness of their hulls makes them look unreal. What with the foam and the spray, they're not sailing anymore, they're flying over a quilted eiderdown. I don't even know if they have crews, or if they're ghost ships, escaped from the clipper races of the past. It's hard to keep track of them because of the enormous waves which hide even their masts.

You all right, Nicolas? No ships?'

Gliksman's cruel question brings me back to sad reality. I've been lookout since 10 a.m. and had practically forgotten our situation. The discomfort of the 'bib', the wetness of my clothes, the raging Atlantic, the sudden violent gusts of wind, had all given way to this race between two white three-masters. How long have I been daydreaming? Five or ten minutes, perhaps more, perhaps less? I could see these boats from another century with my eyes wide open. But it wasn't a kind of unconscious delirium. From staring at the crests of the waves, I thought for a moment that I saw a shape.

There was nothing there, but I deliberately fixed my mind on this fleeting vision and constructed a dream out of this image. For the second time in just over twenty-four hours I've tried to escape from this floating prison and almost succeeded. The return to reality seems even worse inasmuch as there is no means of preparing an escape attempt!

Nervously and physically this first night in our life-raft will be the worst because, like the day before, we must deal with the waves, for the fear of capsize is twice as bad. Chance encounters with salt water would certainly be a more serious matter in his starless night than in daylight. Gliksman has warned us before napping, 'Sleep with one eye open. We must expect to find ourselves in the drink at any moment.' Which idea I rejected, saying, 'It would be preferable to do anything to avoid it.' Which is why whoever's on watch doesn't hesitate to wake the others up to order them to counterbalance. Every muscle in the body is subjected to this hard exercise. They're tensed to the extreme at the moment of impact of the wave, and relaxed immediately after, to become completely amorphous as soon as sleep returns, then stiff again, and so on till morning. We still have to bail out and sponge again and again to be dry, and without much result for the bottoms of our oilskin trousers hold water and it's impossible to empty them. Gliksman alone manages to contort himself and get a sponge between his oilskin and his cotton underpants, but to do so he has to crush a pair of legs or twist an arm. Such moments reveal the possibility of establishing a hierarchy of each person's capacity to endure pain. Denis, the youngest, certainly suffers the most. The term 'delicate' has no more meaning in our rubber ring. All the same, he's the one who could be described as relatively 'delicate'. He's very slender, hasn't an ounce of fat. His bones are so lacking in protection that the least weight applied to his ankles, shins or shoulders causes him to cry out in pain and brings an automatic reproach from his father who doesn't miss the chance to point out that 'we're all in the same boat.' However, Alain Gliksman himself tends to protest when one of us treads on his foot or leg while trying to get his balance. His protests are disguised as statements: 'That's my foot you're standing on', or again, 'My ankle's stuck.' His self-control enables him not to let out a cry of pain which, in other circumstances, would be followed by a curse or a rude remark. We each have our own method. Mine leads to misinterpretation from the start. When the pain becomes unendurable I hold my breath, grit my teeth and steel my muscles; then, when I start to need air I breathe deeply and begin again. I can still feel the pain, but I no longer have any physical means of expressing it. Nevertheless, when I spit the air out of my lungs, I let out a little sigh of relief which Gliksman interprets as a plaintive groan. Olivier pulls sufficiently eloquent faces, but doesn't speak. A couple of times we hear him simply asking politely, 'Would you mind moving your leg a little?' Alain is disconcerting: he gives no sign, whatever his place or position. He seems not to feel pain. Sometimes we have to convince him to arrange his position better. All our suggestions are cut short with his inevitable 'Great'.

The little light has got gradually dimmer and dimmer and now it's gone out completely. We're in the dark and totally lose any idea of length or breadth: depending on whether we're half-reclining or curled up the 'bib' seems large or small, so that we become incapable of guessing its outline. At the moment of falling asleep it's very tempting to try and stretch out completely, but the impossibility of doing it forces resignation, and a frustration that nearly breeds claustrophobia. This feeling of suffocation, coupled with the desire to stretch out, will gradually fade as the nights go by, but this Monday morning it's unbearable. I'm waiting for daybreak as deliverance for listening to the waves breaking, without seeing them, is a real nightmare. *This* should be called hell: to suffer a punishment with no possibility of defending oneself. If it was only a matter of suffering while waiting for it to be over, but we have to struggle unceasingly to prevent our sentence becoming capital. After 'We must stick it out', the second *leitmotiv* will be: 'What have we done to deserve such punishment?' Someone or other will ask this unanswerable question each time the weather worsens. Tonight it's Gliksman who mutters it while bailing, causing me to do an internal review of the mistakes in my life – the troubles I may have caused some people, the hurt I've given to others – but honestly, I can't find anything that justifies this 'punishment'. Gales are frequent enough in the Atlantic but the length of this one – now six days without letup – passes the bounds of ordinary weather. Let's not start talking about God. We're five atheists and couldn't accept that. But there has to be some explanation for this string of bad luck: the storm since our departure, the capsize, the fact that the trimaran began to sink when logically it was unsinkable, the overturning of the liferaft, and still the gale. Yet we're all alive. If we were destined to die, we'd be dead already. Alain and I would have been drowned in the stern cabin; Olivier would have been carried off by the waves; Alain and Denis Gliksman wouldn't have been able to free the raft and would have been trapped in the survival capsule when the trimaran sank. So why keep us alive if not to save us finally? This is a strangely mystical problem for our Cartesian minds and has still not been elucidated by dawn.

The arrival of the sun allows hope of a first calm day. The wind's been falling for an hour, but the waves are even more dangerous. They no longer have flat crests and sometimes break without the help of gusts of wind. The troughs are no longer so deep but the swell is longer, increasing the run of each breaker. About 8 a.m. one of them lifts us up. Gliksman's trying to work out our course mentally; Alain and Denis are napping; Olivier's just finished his watch and I'm getting ready to take over – so no one's looking outside. Suddenly the 'bib' is lifted up. It heels over to 45° as if carried by an unknown force, and charges off at an insane speed. Nothing can stop her. She tears along, half out of the water, as fast as if she had an outboard motor. Gliksman pales and the five of us look at one another questioningly. The 'bib' is planing on top of a breaker like a surfboard and she stays there. The drogue isn't braking her – it must have got twisted. We throw ourselves against the upper float to prevent our improvised surfboard from tipping over, aware that if we go over the crest, we'll be rolled like a piece of pastry. As suddenly as it caught us up, this monstrous wave lets us go, proceeding on its mad course across the Atlantic. Sticking my head outside, I see it disappearing as if our ride together was just a game.

The compass needle wavers between 0° and 020°; the raft's continuing its drift towards the northeast and the sky clears. It's no longer streaked and full of huge grey clouds but dotted with puffy white ones. By mid-morning the wind picks up again, but these first brief glimpses of the sun change the look of the sea: it seems more docile. The waves are less terrifying in the perfect visibility. I take the opportunity of slipping myself half outside. The smell inside is beginning to get me down. It seems that the technique I worked out the previous day of relieving myself in my trousers has made converts. It's impossible to risk doing it overboard, so all night we've been using my solution. Although the method has the advantage of warming up your legs for a few minutes, it also has the disadvantage after several repetitions of producing a foul smell. Mixed with the smell of rubber, it's very disagreeable. I don't know if I have a stronger sense of smell than my companions, but they don't seem worried by this atmosphere of ammoniated effluent. They won't react till later, in the afternoon, when we'll all agree to put an end to this rather childish practice. Weather permitting, we'll 'top up the ocean' on our knees on the two floats. But when this is too risky we'll use a bailer kept for the purpose. Only Olivier remains convinced of the heating value of the first method and continues to use it for four days. For a while it's a favourite subject for discussion: 'the kid who's wet himself' produces laughs. But four days later, Olivier will have all the symptoms of ammonia poisoning.

We begin the second morning with a vitamin biscuit, feeling that we really deserve it. Taking advantage of what seems to be the beginning of a lull, Gliksman takes stock of the survival rations and discovers that in a single day we've eaten nearly all the contents of the first bag. At this rate we could only last for three or four days, and that's not what you could call 'sticking it out'. If we only eat a quarter of a biscuit daily, we'll have enough for a week. Imagining the worst, and knowing that with water the young human body can survive for about three weeks, depending on the circumstances and physical condition, that pushes back a fatal outcome to more than two weeks.

Olivier suggests improving our chances by an attempt at fishing. He spends a minute looking at the material we have found in the raft and then passes sentence: 'I won't.' The end of the line is made of a nylon thread that can't be more than a micron thick, with five hooks attached which couldn't catch a tiddler on the banks of the Marne. The two spare hooks are slightly bigger and might just be strong enough to catch a mackerel in the English Channel. And yet the dorado are still with us. I find them very appetising, and despite Olivier's views I throw out the line. The reputedly voracious fish swim backwards and forwards within two centimetres of the hooks without paying the least attention. Denis fears that the hooks might puncture the rubber and his father adds his weight to the argument: even supposing I can catch one, we've nothing to kill it with; the raft's floating knife has a rounded blade only 3 centimetres long. The struggles of this 60 centimetre fish would damage the raft and cause painful wounds. If the swell improves we might possibly haul in the sea anchor to see if its close mesh has caught any plankton.

The reminder of this method of feeding a castaway, recommended by Alain Bombard, makes us want to profit from any of his other ideas that might be relevant to our situation, but the balance sheet is discouraging. His *Hérétique* was boat-shaped, not an unsteerable aircraft tyre; the winds were with him and they weren't just any old winds: they were trade winds which carried him straight towards the Antilles; he could fish; finally, and above all, he was physically and morally prepared to live as a castaway.

Gliksman admits that it's this precise point that he finds difficult to accept. In all the time he's been sailing, it had never occurred to him that he might be shipwrecked. 'Up to now I've been one of those people who thought that such things only happened to others.' He is a first-class skipper and can't accept feeling helpless at sea. I can tell that he's as upset as a riding instructor who's fallen off his horse and can't manage to remount in front of his pupils. He analyses *RTL-Timex*'s capsize from every angle and can't understand it. An exceptional wave crossed the path of another. This explanation is incomplete and doesn't satisfy him. Then just when we think he's asleep, he opens his eyes, stares at the bottom of the raft without focussing on anything in particular, and carries on as if he hadn't stopped: 'The floats are a metre too short. If we'd had another metre, we wouldn't have turned over.' Gliksman launches into a demonstration of naval architecture, using his hand as the boat and reinforcing his points with gestures. In our little rubber shelter he gives us a magisterial lesson in physics and geometry, from which he concludes that: 'the supporting polygon isn't big enough' and 'the floats should be lengthened by a metre at the stern to make it more efficient.' Personally, I'm not really open to this kind of demonstration of physics, but I manage to concentrate enough to listen. There's no reason why not. I too have the right to know why I'm here on this drifting raft in the Atlantic Ocean. There are several technical terms I don't understand, but when Gliksman reaches his conclusion I follow the principle – having suffered the practical application. He develops his thesis to the point of feeling sympathy for the other famous skippers who are preparing to take part in the next transatlantic race on trimarans with floats that, in his view, are too short.

This discussion of *RTL-Timex*'s structure reminds me of how she looked and brings the astonishing realization that we didn't even take the time to watch her drift away yesterday. In less than five days I had adopted her as my new home. But there were still hundreds of corners, instruments and techniques to discover. I wanted to learn how to use the radio, how to make an astro fix, how to set a spinnaker, how to plot a course. These were all the techniques I had decided to study the prevous summer by enrolling at a cruising school. On Gliksman's trimaran I would have absorbed them without the least effort. At this moment she must still be floating a few miles away. If we're picked up within the next twenty-four hours she can be rescued with everything in her cabins. The film I took on St George's is what I want back more than my personal effects and papers. One of them was the masterpiece of my life, achieved after a two-hour wait in front of a church as people came out from mass. It showed a brilliantly yellow-clad negro, lighting a cigarette in front of the purple wall of the church! This photo improves in the description to my companions in misfortune. 'Even if only to get that photo back, we must recover the boat.'

It looks as if fine weather's setting in. The waves get smaller. The wind continues dropping. The clouds disperse. Rays of sunlight caress the fabric of the canopy. I'm sitting on the float with half my body outside, recharging myself in the sun like a battery. I'd like to close my eyes for a moment, but it's not the time for sunbathing; I must scan the horizon for a rescue ship. I'm on the edge of the craft and have a nearly 360° sector of vision so within roughly 10° or 20° I can cover the whole horizon. I've opened my anorak and my wet clothes are warming up. If the sun stays out we'll be able to dry our things. Little by little, I take off my anorak and duvet waistcoat, but I prefer to let my pullover and tee-shirt dry on me. I open two of the flaps so that the others can enjoy this beneficial warmth. Denis takes off his oilskins, then his anorak and tracksuit. He's stripped to the waist. But the relief due to the disappearance of irritations caused by wet synthetic fabrics gives way to the discomfort of having undressed too quickly and he begins shivering. He puts his wet tracksuit back on, hoping to stop the shivering, but it only makes it worse, for he's overcome with trembling, his face whitens, his teeth chatter. He just manages to mumble 'I don't feel well', and we have to put all his wet clothes back on and roll him up in the aluminium sheet. This shivering lasts a quarter of an hour before Denis falls asleep, worn out by this new trial.

The sea isn't a mirror, far from it, but compared to the previous days it's practically calm. We don't have to screw up our eyes to scan the horizon any more. Neither do we have to fling ourselves against the floats to deaden the shock of waves. Our bodies can rest, our stiffness relax and our minds wander. We can speak without shouting and even try to sleep without fear of a brutal awakening. My jaw hurts from having gritted my teeth continuously for forty-eight hours. I have to grit them again from time to time, as if to force them down into their sockets, in order to reduce this dull ache. We feel the effects of this sunny calm. Obviously we'd hesitate to go out in a raft from an Atlantic or Mediterranean beach, and the lifeguards would have the red 'dangerous to bathe' flag out, but for us it's like a tropical summer after a Canadian winter. It's also the source of a whole string of new hopes. If the sun stays out we'll be physically less tested and will be able to reduce our biscuit ration further. And although we'll have to drink more, we have enough reserves to envisage holding out for more than a month. But if the sun really stays out and the sea calm, we won't need to 'keep going' for the perfectly simple reason that we'll be picked up! Our chances of being picked up have increased enormously because of the perfect visibility, which considerably multiplies the probability of seeing or being seen. The 'bib' is no longer hidden in troughs, and its reflective strips now serve a purpose. Perhaps an airline jet might spot a tiny point and not lose it among the breakers, if there aren't any. Then there's the wreckage of *RTL-Timex*: she too has become easier to spot, even just below the surface. Furthermore, the people who are expecting us in New York will start worrying now that the storm is over. Up till now they've had cause enough to think we would make little progress, but our delay is no longer explicable and this will cause a search to be mounted within a day or two. The search zone can't be enormous, for having been shipwrecked 150 miles from Bermuda, we must be more or less 300 to 500 miles from the American coast. Apparently we're only drifting slightly eastwards. Since the compass is still showing a NNE route, we're still in the logical search zone. Even if the search planes don't spot us, they'll certainly pick up the wreck of *RTL-Timex*. I remember following, from my Paris office, the operation organized to find Alain Colas, reported missing during the Route de Rhum. French Navy planes flew over hundreds and hundreds of square miles for two months without seeing a thing.

My companions' enthusiasm seems a bit excessive to me and to slow them down I remind them of those sad hours and the negative outcome. But on this day nothing can tarnish their hopes; Gliksman, supported by Denis and Alain, explains that the methods employed by the U.S. Coast Guards are very different from the French patrols. 'They don't go round and round an approximate position. In our case they have a precise location: the Coast Guard frigate we talked to during our second day. Her captain will have logged our position, so all the search planes have to do is go to this location and start flying in gradually larger concentric circles till they find us. It'll take two or three days at the most.' But to get there, the people in New York must start panicking a bit! If my colleague from *L'Express* is dying to get on board she'll tear off to the port authorities for news, as I did in Bermuda. Alain and Olivier have more faith that the crew of Olivier Kersauson's *Kriter IV* will give the alert. Besides, yachting journalists are waiting on the quay at New York for our double departure. And furthermore, even if no alert comes from the United States, there are plenty of people in France who are going to get worried. Our families, the RTL staff, and the Timex management will all be concerned about our fate. Once again Alain terminates the discussion: 'They won't have time to get worried, given that we'll be taking a hot shower on board a freighter or a Russian submarine tonight!'

The dorado are still there, and I'm sure that I could catch them easily if I only had a harpoon, or even a simple pointed penknife. I remark, for the others' benefit, 'I have the feeling that the bastards are taunting us.' Gliksman replies, 'I wonder who's going to be first to eat who. But I advise them not to have any illusions.'

He shoes his head out mechanically for a quick look. When anyone of us scans the horizon he has a quick look too just for form's sake. Like yesterday, he hesitates a long time before announcing: 'A ship – there!' Alain leaps on the box of flares, while Denis gets out the distress beacon. This second ship is a lot closer than the first and coming at us presenting the bow quarter. Her deck is covered with pipework which stands out perfectly against the now almost clear blue sky. Alain's just set off a rocket flare. This time we all stay very calm, as if we sense that this tanker won't see us. I tell myself, 'If she doesn't see us, perhaps she'll hear the radio or the explosion of the rocket.' A second red flare climbs into the sky. Gliksman asks Alain not to fire any more, his tone perfectly calm with no trace of disappointment. Already we can't see the tanker's decks as she continues on her course having slightly veered to the east. We watch her disappearing until she's no more than a tiny point on the horizon, as we watched yesterday's ship.

Denis tirelessly continues transmitting 'Maydays' with the radio beacon. The quarter hour which follows our brief encounter with the tanker is full of our sarcastic but not despairing comments. She's the second ship to cross our path in twenty-four hours: this confirms Gliksman's theory that we're not far from the shipping routes. So it's advisable to keep up the lookout above all at night. In fact watches will be doubled up to increase efficiency with a lookout at each end of the raft to cover the 360° horizon. Besides, it's easier to stay awake at night in twos.

Alain immediately puts this decision into practice by taking up a position at the opposite end of the raft. By pushing down on the tent arch, we can see each other and a silly dialogue begins:

'Fancy seeing you here. I thought you were on Gliksman's trimaran.'

'No. As you see, I prefer inflatable rafts.'

'Well well, what a small world.'

'What are you doing this evening?'

Etc, etc.

Looking at Alain, I notice that his beard hasn't grown. He's beardless and his almost dry blond hair is as clean as if he'd washed it the previous day. He's quite presentable while Gliksman, Olivier and I are beginning to look like castaways. Denis hasn't got a beard either, but Olivier and Gliksman look pitiful, their cheeks hollow with a growing black shadow. Their wet hair makes them look even thinner and their complexions are greyish. Still, our health isn't a problem. Since Denis's little alarm, the crew hasn't complained of anything except painful jaws and a few aches. Neither hunger nor, surprisingly, thirst have upset our stomachs or dried our throats. The worst thing about this second day is the inactivity.

This moment of respite is disconcerting after the

hours and hours of struggling with the waves and bailing out the bottom of the raft. There's nothing to 'do', no sailing, no fishing. Writing perhaps? But the pen Gliksman hands me refuses to give out the tiniest drop of ink and anyway the only paper we rescued is soaked. The bill of sale of the boat and her insurance papers are both unreadable. The ink has run, giving them the appearance of canvases in the Museum of Modern Art. Only Gliksman's, Olivier's and Denis's passports have kept a few visas unstained. Gliksman suggests a few party games. Still seated on the edge of the float, I pretend not to hear, to avoid participating. I've never liked such pastimes even when I was a child at primary or secondary school; I found them a bit pointless and ridiculous. On days when nothing much is happening in the reporters' corner of an editorial office, this type of amusement helps fill the time, but I always find a good reason not to be one of the players. I have the same reaction here. Inside, Gliksman is explaining the rules of 'word chain', which consists of finding a word or an expression which begins with the last syllable of the preceding word. From my corner I follow their attempts to find a word with a beginning that follows on from the word just said. Thinking about my reaction, I find it even sillier than theirs. Here we are alone in the middle of the Atlantic. No one can see or hear us. We've got nothing better to do than sit and wait for a ship to deign to come and pick us up, and I'm sitting here making pronouncements about what is ridiculous. Ridiculous in relation to who and what, given that values aren't the same here? I must think differently, and accept what I refused on land. We have to reverse our life style in every way. Our motives are different: we must use anything that can help us stay alive. We can't stop our bladders for the sake of modesty; we can't stop bailing out because we're tired; we can't cry because we're afraid, or eat a biscuit because we're hungry. So, if I need to play 'word chain' to get my brain working, I haven't got the right to refuse for fear of ridicule. Besides, I *feel* like playing now!

The game isn't a great success. The memory of the last ship is doubtless too fresh in our minds for us to be able to concentrate on this futile occupation. But Gliksman insists and suggests another game: 'If...'. He explains: 'Four of us choose a person or a thing and the fifth must find out what it is by giving a sequence of ideas. For example, *if* the Eiffel Tower were a thing, reply: it would be big, etc.'

Olivier puts a stop to this before it's even begun: 'If I understand this right, someone has to go out while the others choose their person? In which case I'd like a transfer to another boat. I'm fed up with getting wet.' After this outburst of laughter, Gliksman gives up his inclination for games and falls back into a restful sleep. More and more clouds are racing across the sky. They're flooding over the horizon like the jackpot from a slot-machine. Alain is worried by my observation and asks if they look like the piped potato puree on *coquille St Jacques*. As I can't make up my mind, he comes to look for himself. He's obviously relieved and explains that if this had been the case, we would have had to cope with a hurricane. We may well have escaped a hurricane, but the wind gets up again and the sky again fills with grey clouds. The sea is still pretty calm, but this can't last if the wind keeps up.

Four hours after we saw the tanker Olivier bounds onto his knees, screws up his eyes and asks if I can see anything in the direction he's pointing. It takes a whole minute before we decide to act. Rummaging in the canvas bag, Denis has just discovered a signalling mirror which we hadn't known existed until now. While I wave the aluminium sheet, he tries to aim the reflection from the mirror at this third ship. She's really a long way off, but is bow-on. Will she come towards us? Alain puts forward this theory, which doubles my heart rate and I sense excites the others. Gliksman tries calling on the radio, but it's more to give himself something to do than in any hope of a response. Its batteries are running out and we wonder whether this accursed orange box has ever worked. Yet we did once try it out on *RTL-Timex* from the after cabin to the boat's own radio, and it worked. Still, the big difference between the two or three metres that separated us then and the forty or so kilometres distance between us and this ship today leaves doubt about the usefulness of our transmitting box. The aluminium sheet's blowing about in the wind. It should make a superb target, if not to see at least on the ship's radar. If this one doesn't see us, I'll change my theory. We can now make her out abeam, but it's quite impossible to tell if she's a freighter, a passenger liner, or a tanker. Five minutes later she changes course and disappears over the horizon like the others. Each time it's the same story: just when we think she's coming towards us, the ship changes course. We start wondering if they're making a detour after spotting us. This idle question suddenly deepens into a serious one. The many recent cases of tankers grounding on the Brittany coast while trying to avoid the statutory traffic lanes in order to save fuel, hence money, are hardly reassuring. Is the captain of a 200,000 ton tanker going to stop his ship, which will take easily a quarter of an hour, then back up, put out a launch and thus lose thousands of francs just to rescue us? We end up collectively convincing ourselves of the unlikelihood of such an attitude: a seaman couldn't abandon five other shipwrecked seamen. But inside I'm sure that the others, like me, have doubts at this moment about the noble legendary laws of the sea. The sea no longer belongs to seamen, but to money.

Which doesn't stop us keeping a lookout that night. Seeing two boats in a single day augurs well for the future. Meanwhile the wind's got up again and our drift has changed. We're now headed south, not north, which won't take us nearer the American coast and reduces our chances of getting into the main shipping lanes to New York. At dusk, I report to Gliksman that the setting sun looks very yellow and he pulls a face and asks if it looks pale or bright. The rays are widely spread and Gliksman's face gets worse: 'We're in for another battering tonight.'

The night watches are set in twos, as arranged, and limited to an hour. Gliksman and Olivier settle down one at each end of the 'bib', which allows them to slip their heads through the flaps. To avoid letting the cold and the water in, they only pull the flaps aside and close them again as quickly as they can after each observation.

Olivier is the first to taste salt again. At the exact moment he puts his head through the flap, a shower of spray crashes over the raft, more or less marking the end of the truce which has lasted a bit more than five hours. For within ten minutes we have to get out the bailers and start work again. The water gets in on one side or on all four at once, depending on the strength of the waves. After a brief calculation we're able to pick out the place least likely to receive an icy shower. At first it's given to each person in turn; then to anyone who hasn't got an oilskin jacket; finally to anyone who's physically in need of it. We actually manage to get some sleep during this third night as castaways, and the second on our rubber contraption: short periods of deep sleep with occasional nightmares. Alain's the first to share his dreams. About midnight, twenty minutes after finishing his watch, he suddenly sits up with his eyes half open, seeing nothing in particular, and starts shouting 'We must change the spinnaker, but the steering gear's locked up! Who locked up the steering gear? I can't get forward!' Denis and I turn towards him taken aback. He seems so sure of what he's saying that for a moment we wonder if it's we who are dreaming. We force him to lie down again, then try to persuade him that he's been dreaming and must go back to sleep. But he's visibly angry and mutters incomprehensibly before calming down. He doesn't wake up and the following morning can remember nothing, not even the dream that angered him so.

Later the same night I alert the whole crew. I suddenly get up and scream 'Ship ahead to starboard!' Everyone rushes to the openings without seeing anything. I hear a question from the panic-stricken Gliksman: 'Where, where is there a ship?' I repeat 'Ahead to starboard. Isn't that clear enough?' Denis clarifies the situation, explaining that I'm asleep and dreaming, which infuriates me. 'I'm *not* dreaming. I'm not mad. I *saw* a ship there, *ahead to starboard*!' I continue to insist but begin to realize that in fact I've been dreaming. Yet I'm only vaguely aware of it, can't control my words, and continue getting angry before falling asleep again. When they tell me about this 'sleep-walking' episode the following morning, I find it impossible to explain that I was perfectly lucid, but simply couldn't control my words. I heard myself saying things, I knew I was dreaming, but I couldn't stop myself. Furthermore I really was angry, thinking they were taking me for a fool. On these two occasions, our attacks of sleep-walking caused concern, but we got used to them until they became a joke. The only thing was that each time our voices sounded so definite that whoever witnessed the scene hesitated to decide that we were dreaming.

On waking up, happy that the night's over again at last, I have the unpleasant surprise of discovering that my hands are covered with blisters. I find little spots on all my finger joints. Olivier has the same symptoms, but he only has three or four much smaller spots. The others have absolutely nothing. I'm afraid I might be going to have an attack of boils, but I force myself not to think about it. Although they're slightly painful, what I decide to think of as unimportant 'hurts' will be forgotten within a few hours. On the other hand, we've all got another pain in the area of our behinds, that we can't ignore. Denis is the first to complain that he can't sit down. He pulls a face each time he moves and can't find a position where it doesn't hurt, yet can't explain whether the pain is on the skin or in the muscle. He feels every wave that strikes the raft through the rubber, and can't stop himself swearing. It's even worse when he tries to support himself on his elbows. The combined effects of seawater and the chafing of his synthetic fibre sleeves have rubbed his skin off. The flesh of his elbow is raw. We all have the same problem. The seawater and various bits of our clothes have attacked our flesh, rubbing the skin off in several places. Rummaging around in the meagre first-aid kit, Alain finds the antiseptic mercurochrome ointment. He applies the salve to all the affected parts and, not wishing to waste any, rubs the last off on his face. But he was in such a hurry to finish that he didn't take the time to look at the colour of this ointment and when he turns back towards us can't understand why we all laugh. We hand him the signalling mirror so that he can enjoy the spectacle himself. Without knowing what he was doing, he's given himself authentic warpaint like a real redskin. Apart from its beautiful decorative effects, and after some initial burning sensation, this ointment calms the irritation. Unfortunately a thumb-sized tube is clearly too small to serve everyone. We no longer know what position to adopt to avoid contact between some surface or other and our painful areas. The 'bib' suddenly seems more demanding. Sometimes we have to hold ourselves back from violently elbowing the person who's just touched a painful spot.

It's the third day, and the waves continue their plentiful spraying. We've hardly hung up the mugs to start sponging when a new shower of spray means we have to begin again. The chain is reorganized: Gliksman and Gouedard bail, Olivier and I tip the water overboard, while Denis is lookout. On my side the wind is pushing the canopy against the float. Each time I push the mug between the fabric and the rubber tube, I scrape the top of my hand. My blisters burst and each movement tears off a bit of skin. It stings and burns, but I put up with it, remembering that seawater is supposed to sterilize wounds. And in fact the wounds will be sterilized, but get horribly deep. My forearms are covered with a kind of red spot that looks like a symptom of venereal disease rather than seawater sores. Due to these effects of seawater on various parts of our bodies, bailing sessions on this third day are punctuated with short periods of scratching which only make the itching worse.

Fed up with having to spend too much time untying the bailers, which are my responsibility, Denis decides to teach me a few nautical knots. His knots are as easy to undo as they are effective. My basic bowline knot isn't good enough for him and for a quarter of an hour he tries to explain his to me. By the end of the lesson I've forgotten my knot without having learned his, and mine is getting less and less effective and harder and harder to undo. As this lesson ends, the 'bib' reminds us that it

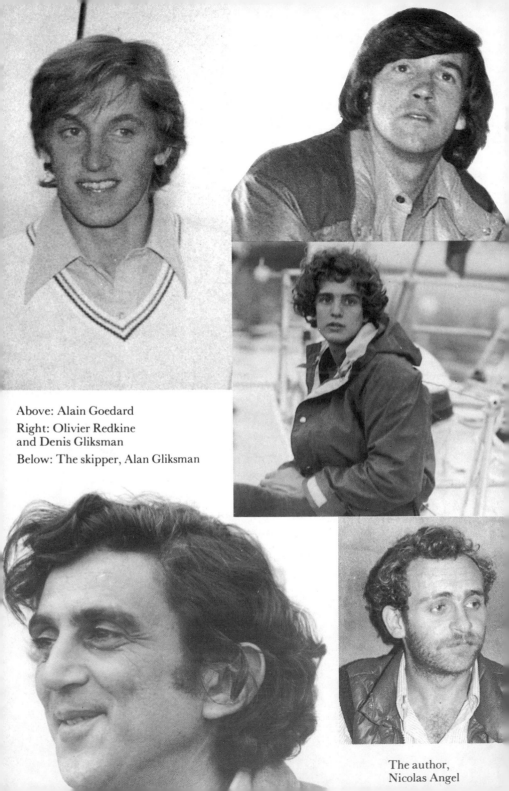

Above: Alain Goedard

Right: Olivier Redkine
and Denis Gliksman

Below: The skipper, Alan Gliksman

The author,
Nicolas Angel

The member of the *Afran Dawn*'s crew who took the photo on the jacket of this book, on the tanker's deck.

Tears of reunion on Sunday, April 22, 1979

We certainly owed it to the Bib to bring it back to Paris.

Nicolas Angel, Georges Nacam and Bernard Gimmic experimenting in the Mediterranean with a 'navigable' type of liferaft, the NACAM 300.

can't withstand heavy seas. It's lifted up by the waves as on the first day and begins to turn over. It rises up to the vertical and then falls again, just as the canopy arch touches the water. Luckily our counterbalancing system has become a reflex and *in extremis* prevents complete capsize. The combined action of waves and gusts of wind takes us twice to the edge of catastrophe. We check that everything's properly stowed, and the only other thing to do is bail and sponge faster.

After this second moment of peril I notice Denis's whitened face and staring look. He's been visibly terrified and for the first time draws near to his father. Gliksman's behaviour never betrays his parental relationship, as I already noted on the trimaran. Nothing's changed during the three days on the raft and this has left me skeptical. But this time the mask has fallen. Like us, Denis is in a state of shock since our two near-capsizes, and he's come to fall asleep on his father's shoulder. Seeing them side by side at last, one might imagine that they've been reunited after a long separation, and I can't help feeling relieved. Olivier's shrug of the shoulders and Alain's tender smile confirm this feeling. There's no need to say anything, we all understand. Personally, I can see my own father's image in this father on whose shoulder Denis can take refuge. His features come into my mind, I can almost hear his voice, but I quickly try to blot this thought out, because it sticks in my throat. As on each occasion that I've felt memories surging up, I force myself to talk to avoid giving in to them. And our two near-capsizes are an excellent topic of conversation to pull us out of our nostalgic thoughts.

'If there hadn't been five of us, she would have capsized.'

Our weight of roughly 300 kilos, thrown against the windward side of the raft, was just enough to balance her. You don't have to be a technician to understand that a single man couldn't have done it. It's the first time that we've thought deeply about Alain Colas's disappearance, although he's haunted us since the capsize. How could Alain have had the time to get his liferaft out if *Manureva* had overturned as quickly as *RTL-Timex*? If the raft got caught up underneath the trimaran, one man would have had very little hope of freeing it. But if he had been able to embark in the raft, even given the best possible physical condition we can't believe that he could have survived the successive capsizes. Like everyone else, we can't conceive of dying in a liferaft. We thought that all we had to do, once in this rubber ring, was wait to be picked up, without having to struggle physically to save our skins. The revelation is confirmed by more treacherous assaults during the long days and nights which follow.

The wind's changed again. We're heading NNE as on the first day. Olivier and Alain try to cover their bare feet with the aluminium sheet. The wind's colder tonight and water's cooled down a few degrees. The evening promises to be trying. We're more highly motivated than on the previous nights because this has been the first day that we've seen no ships and this worries us. Could we have left the shipping routes? We can't stick our heads out during the night, but have to be content with quickly opening the canopy flaps and then closing them again. They're getting slacker and slacker because of the action of the wind which has been pushing them out of shape for three days. When the water forces its way in, now it doesn't only wet those immediately under the openings but also those who thought they were sheltered. Curiously, wherever Olivier and I choose to be, we get hit by spray. We just have to stick our noses out for a wave to slap us across the face. It's like a bad joke in a cartoon film. Bailing out becomes almost pleasant in this cold as it warms us up and stops cramp. I can feel the cold through my boots and wet socks, and wonder how Olivier and Alain can stand it. Gliksman, Denis and I suggest sharing out our boots and socks, but their reply is categorical: they don't want to! The water in the bottom of the 'bib' warms up with the heat of our bodies and the canopy cuts out the wind, but each time anyone moves, even slightly, his feet are re-exposed to the draught and the whole arrangement has to be reworked. This renewed physical assault changes the subject of our dreams. In his usual perfectly clear voice, Alain says to Denis, 'Great, you make me a nice hot coffee and I'll go back up on deck.'

Denis wonders if it's another joke, but Alain's asleep with his fists clenched. Later I interpret Olivier's mumblings as 'Close the door – there's a draught.' *I'm* woken up by a freezing wave and, still half asleep, say to Alain, 'Where are the three people we picked up?' followed by 'They must have gone back to their raft.' This time I react to his astonishment with 'Forget it, I was dreaming.'

The sun's hardly up before I'm out on the float, only too happy that the night's over – another cold wet night with no ships. I'm far from being superstitious, but a little mental calculation has led me to the discovery of a date (today's) that is hardly pleasing. To be sure that I'm not mistaken, I put it to the others in the form of a riddle:

'What's the day today?'
'Friday.'
'Friday the what?'
'Friday the 13th!'

In Gliksman's view nothing worse could possibly happen to us, given what we've already suffered. Alain outdoes him by assuring us that Friday the 13th is also a lucky date and that without doubt we'll get picked up that day. 'Moreover,' he adds eagerly, 'the wind's falling and the sea will soon calm.' He's hardly finished speaking when a gust of wind flattens the canopy and an enormous wave refills the raft. Everyone exlaims in disgust when we take off the sheet to begin bailing again. The ammoniated effluent contained all night beneath the sheet escapes violently, burning our throats and upsetting even Olivier. He hasn't dared open his oilskin jacket for twenty-four hours and has seemed embarrassed and moved as little as possible. This morning he admits that this practice really is disagreeable and decides to use the 'green' mug like the rest of us. As for the *other* problem of a similar order, the cold and perhaps fear have stopped us from thinking about it. A sort of 'vaso-constriction', no doubt.

Alain has just slipped his feet into the sleeves of the quilted jacket that's so wet no one wanted to put it on. Seeing that Alain can't stand being barefoot anymore, Gliksman once again suggests his socks. He confronts Alain's refusal by explaining that one can stand the cold better at forty-six than at twenty-four. He addresses this remark equally to Olivier and Denis, but I get the impression that he's not including me in the group. It's true that people usually think I'm older than I am, perhaps because of my moustache. I explain eagerly that I'm twenty-four too. I couldn't have succeeded better if I'd dealt him a blow with a hammer, for Gliksman gapes: he obviously thought I was older. In fact, like the others, I'm the same generation as his son.

It's midday. We've just eaten our quarter biscuit when a new shower wets us through. A wave entered directly via a hole opened by the wind. What we feared has happened: the sea anchor's gone. The raft is turning round in circles and the waves are hitting from all directions. To keep it balanced, we get down on all fours in the middle, all facing the same way, and begin a hellish roundabout. If a wave comes from the right, we fling ourselves onto the right float. If from the left, we do it again to the left. Meanwhile, we must replace the sea anchor. The radio beacon's batteries are dead and so it gets hung on the end of the 'parcel string' which serves as an anchor warp. The respite is short-lived. This peculiar sea anchor snaps after an hour and we have to begin again. Waves are coming at us from all sides and we must find something else to brake the raft and hold it on to the waves. Gliksman empties the bag containing his ship's papers and it suffers the same fate as the beacon. Half an hour later all that's left of it is the handles. We can still use the flare box as a sea anchor; after that we'll have the jerry cans of fresh water. The box holds! It doesn't brake the raft enough, but it's made of an unbreakable plastic moulding. We add the empty water tins (which we were hoping to use as a radar reflector) to make the box heavier and more effective. To be on the safe side we double up the warp, which is showing renewed signs of weakness, with the grabropes. By sunset this contraption is finally in place.

5

Death Without Goodbye

G liksman wasn't wrong: yesterday evening's yellow sunset kept its promise. We haven't slept very much and our clothes need wringing out. The water temperature is still dropping, the wind increasing. The completely ruptured canopy flaps let in the least ripple. We don't even have time to hang our bailers up on the inside grabropes this Saturday morning. We can't manage to turn the tap of this cold shower off. Olivier drops one of the sponges overboard in the rush. The loss of this deluxe tool brings about an improvement in our drying technique. Stage one is to reduce the number of risky and unnecessary actions by emptying the bailers and sponges into a container which, once full, is then tipped overboard. This precaution reduces the risk of losing the second sponge, which up to now has been wrung out directly outside. From now on, to be doubly sure this object is also tied either to its user's wrist or to one of the grabropes with an anorak cord. We can't allow its loss for it's vital for the maintenance of our meagre comfort. For stage two, I turn tailor or sailmaker. There's only one way to close up the flaps: sew up the openings. Using a safety-pin and a little round file that Alain's just found in his pocket, I make holes along the full height of the flap edges. With anorak cords and the remains of a roll of bandage I accomplish a magnificent lacing-up operation which wins my companions' admiration. Olivier comes to sit immediately underneath it, convinced that it's watertight. But the arrival of a new shower demonstrates its inadequacy. I double the lacing, which logically shouldn't let in the least drop now. Thousands and thousands of drops still get in — so much for logic. This new makeshift repair session throws us into an uncontrollable rage. Whoever designed this floating contraption deserves to be called every name under the sun. We dream of putting him in one of his own products in the middle of the Atlantic. We even envisage exhibiting the raft at the next Paris Boat Show, and asking visitors to get inside while buckets of water are thrown over them so that they can understand our anger. This half an hour letting off steam gives us an appetite and Gliksman hands round quarters of biscuits. After five days on this diet we find them almost tasty. But Alain sets off memories of civilized food by talking about how much he misses real coffee and hot buttered toast. Curiously, our imaginations recreate the smell of fresh coffee and the taste of salted butter. This is followed by the conjuring up of the flavour of a whole lot of simple dishes. Denis dreams of a steak, Olivier of a chicken leg, Gliksman of spaghetti, and me of an enormous American cheesecake of the type I gorged myself on in Bermuda. As a result of this discussion we all feel nostalgic and decide not to talk about cooking anymore. But after this the flavour of Breton butter keeps coming to excite my taste buds.

We haven't seen a ship now for two days and three nights. Gliksman is working out our estimated drift on a map found among the ship's papers the previous evening, for he thinks that within twenty-four hours we'll be back in the shipping routes where we were on Wednesday. This prediction proves right. A little after 2 p.m. Olivier interrupts a discussion to say calmly 'Look, a ship.' We're so unconvinced of the truth of this statement that we ask him not to make jokes about this subject. Olivier is already on his feet crying 'But I'm not joking – she's enormous!' She'd been hidden by the waves till now, but she's only 200 to 300 metres away. We can clearly see her deck loaded with containers and the dark strip of her name, without being able to read it. This one can't not see us.

Gliksman decides to use flares. The container ship is abeam. She's come a little closer. The first flare goes straight up, but the smoke bomb which Gliksman has just opened refuses to ignite. Olivier has taken off his yellow oilskin and is waving it about over his head. The container ship continues on her way without coming any nearer. Alain lets off a second flare while Olivier thinks this is already pointless for the ship hasn't seen us and we're now too far astern in relation to her bridge to have any chance of being seen. I can't believe that we could be so close and not be rescued this time. I practically order Olivier to carry on waving his oilskin. You never know, maybe a sailor has come out for air on the stern deck. She continues to get further away, but Denis is sure that this movement is the beginning of a U-turn. We all hope he's right, but like the others I don't share his conviction. The ship veers slightly to the northwest but continues on her way. I don't understand: if a ship can pass so close to us and not see us, who *can* see us? It means that if the sea doesn't get calm we'll never be picked up. Moreover, from our water level position even *we* lost sight of this floating mountain each time we were in a trough.

We become terribly bitter when we realize that

barely a quarter of an hour's difference and our courses would have crossed: if she'd been going faster; if we'd drifted slower; if the wind had fallen.... This series of suppositions forces us finally to accept our helplessness. With a sail, we could have got nearer. We might even have been able to paddle, if our raft were boat-shaped. As it is there's nothing to be done, nothing but watch her disappearing in the distance and hope that the next one will see us, if there is a next one. Now we must redo the lacing, which didn't survive our excitement.

'Two all.' Alain Gouedard pulls us out of our apathy by giving the score in a new game he's invented: Gliksman's seen two ships, so has Olivier. Whoever wins will be given lunch by the others back in Paris. It seems to us that Alain is as much of a jinx as an optimist. Yet again, he's hardly finished saying that it's getting calmer when a gust punctuates his sentence by practically overturning us. This filthy weather won't let us go; we suffer depression after depression. Cold fronts are followed by warm fronts, the wind turns and then instead of dropping picks up again, and it's warm front, cold front, etc. Gliksman can't – doesn't want to – understand anymore. From time to time he looks at the sky and repeats his refrain of 'I don't believe it. What have we done to deserve it?' Then, as on every occasion that a heavy silence has fallen among us, he takes hold of the situation again, gradually restarting conversation.

We try to deduce the course of the search and rescue operation. Our delay must finally have alerted the people who were expecting us, for they must have realized that if we haven't arrived in New York ten days after our departure from St George's Island, it can only be because we've encountered difficulties. They'll give the alert, if they haven't already, and the planes will soon be taking off. But who would take the initiative to launch such an operation? Gliksman hopes that Marie-Christine, his press secretary, is already in touch with the U.S. Coast Guard. Denis is counting on his mother worrying. Olivier, who's regretting not keeping his parents informed of his least movements and habits, fears that they won't react fast enough. Alain follows more or less the same reasoning: 'I've done so many crazy things, from my trips on a raft in a force 8 to my Channel crossing in my Hobie cat, that even if my parents worry they're convinced that I'll always come through it all right, and they're right.'

Personally, I'm sure that my best 'mate' is working like a madman to find us. My 'mate' being my father. I can't explain why, but I find myself wanting to explain his personality to the others – what he means to me, and I to him. All four professional sailors are used to getting through difficult patches on their own; it's a point of honour for them not to ask for help. They're even hoping to be saved from this raft without crying help! I'm the only one able to admit to the group that I'm counting on the help of someone outside it, and in this case they'll find it easier to accept the idea. Thus I'm convinced that my father will be behind all attempts undertaken to find us. At sixty-three he can't stand not hearing from his son every forty-eight hours, so he won't be able to rest after these six days of silence. Strangely enough, on the eve of my departure he'd said, 'I don't like this. Racing trimarans haven't been perfected yet: they capsize easily.' A premonition, or a legitimate reaction for a father who's worrying about his son? Yet it was *he* who gave me a taste for sailing. *He* who went out in the English Channel in his 420 dinghy when even fishermen stayed in port. *He* who still planes around in his Laser when the *mistral*'s blowing, and *he*, finally, who's always left me free to live my life as I see fit! I'm convinced that he will have already moved heaven and earth to rescue us, and I manage to persuade the others too.

My discourse is interrupted by the raft heeling over at a dangerous angle under the effect of a larger wave than usual. The sea looks like the worst days again: a chaos of crossing waves breaking on all sides, trails of white foam, gusts of wind which flatten the canopy, and an unbearable noise redoubling in intensity. It isn't the cold that paralyses me, or losing my balance that makes me grip the grabropes in my fist, it's *fear*. I'm certain we'll all be dead within half an hour. Denis has perceived my turmoil and I can't stand to look at him. In fact I don't want to see or hear any more. My throat's tight and my neck stiff. I don't want to crack up in front of the others. I won't allow myself; and then, unconsciously no doubt, I don't want to be the first. By pretending to be asleep I cover up my fear and isolate myself from the enmity of the elements, closing my eyes and lying down on my side. Nobody forced me to come on this adventure. I came of my own free will and must accept the consequences right to the end. I'm determined – *me*, the one who sometimes wondered how he'd feel on the day of his death. I was more afraid of physical pain than death itself. Now, today, I'm indifferent to pain. As an adolescent I was driven to consider suicide, like others at that age. The idea of ceasing to live didn't frighten me, since after death there was nothing, nothingness, with no chance of remorse or regrets. But here, if I reject the idea of dying it's for others, for those who are waiting for me. *They* have the right to know that they'll never see me again, and *why* they'll never see me again. My father and mother didn't bring me up and love me twenty-four hours a day for it all to stop, without any way for them to understand. I must have at the very least the chance of dying on a ship after being picked up, with the possibility of writing or leaving a message. I remember a journalist friend saying 'Death at sea is the gentlest end.' How wrong he was: it's certainly the most horrible. To disappear in solitude with no chance to say goodbye to those one loves! For this reason alone, I must keep up appearances, hold on, 'stick it out'. I raise myself up and force myself to look at the sea, to stare at each wave defiantly. Finally, mechanically, I pick up a bailer and begin to participate in the life of the raft again.

We're beginning our sixth night as castaways. Gliksman and Olivier take the first watch and I can sleep. The cold is more and more penetrating and I don't find it easy. We're all piled on top of one another without much care for comfort. Although we're all curled up on half a float, the 'bib' seems twice as small as on the first day. The canopy has sagged to the point that we have to prop it up with a paddle to avoid having to hunch our shoulders. The aluminium sheet, which has protected us till now, is in tatters and hardly covers our feet. Now and again we have to reinflate the two floats and the double bottom, which are getting soft because of the sudden fall in temperature. The last straw is that the sea water battery has finally died, leaving us in total darkness. Those on watch must struggle not to become numb or fall asleep. As soon as one falls asleep, the other must wake him up. Each watches the other continually. We know that even a quarter of an hour's inattention can let a ship go by. The method of checking takes the form of a little question: 'See anything?' followed by the reply: 'If I did, I wouldn't keep it to myself!'

Once again I achieve fame by dreaming aloud. My dream is a mixture of earthly cares and marine problems. Half sitting up and gesticulating, I grumble: 'This is ridiculous. How do you expect me to drive without a windscreen wiper? Besides, I refuse to declutch with sailing boots!' I have no memory at all of this dream the following morning and am quite incapable of recounting my adventures in a car.

At the first light of dawn I take up my observation post as usual. Seated on the float, I enjoy the few feeble rays of sunlight that aren't hidden by clouds. I sarcastically point out that today is the 'Lord's day' and imagine everyday life in Paris. With the six hour time difference French families must be getting lunch ready after a long lie in. There are hot chocolate and *croissants*, perhaps after mass. And then this afternoon they'll go for a walk in the park, or enjoy the luxury of a film in the Champs Elysées. While I, we, are idling about like idiots in the middle of the North Atlantic waiting for a wretched little ship to happen by with a crew who will deign to notice us. I repeat like a cracked record, 'Six days, six days we've been drifting on a Boeing 747 tyre, sometimes north, sometimes south. We've passed four ships. We haven't caught a fish. And we're still alive.' I wonder if this is good or bad luck. If we'd been ship-wrecked more than five days after our departure from New York and in the middle of our transatlantic record attempt, would we have stood the freezing waters of the fiftieth parallel for so long? Moreover, we would have had a sixth passenger in the 'bib', my colleague from *L'Express*, and a woman to boot! Remembering how much trouble I had to get on board as a journalist, I realize that I shouldn't even be here. I spent a whole evening arguing myself on board Gliksman's trimaran in place of another journalist from *L'Équipe*. And what about that plane I missed the first time and just caught the second? Shouldn't I have read all these events as signs? Am I going to end up thinking like a fortune-teller? Must destiny and fate and all those big words that used to make me smile in my cosy little nest in

Paris – must they be given more importance because I'm on a bit of rubber? I ask myself this question honestly, but can't bring myself to reply.

While I'm completing this private little scene the others are beginning to wake up and stir. Denis is already trying to botch up a power system for the interior light with the help of one of the two spare batteries from the torch which has never worked, a safety-pin and some elastic, to make a sort of mini-battery with an efficient switch built in. Olivier has obviously been thinking about fishing, for he gets the gear out of his pocket again and tries to find a way to strengthen it. The dorado are still circling the raft and the little yellow fish has come back to rejoin the group. Up to now, Gliksman has been against our attempts at fishing, but this morning he admits that he'd be glad to eat a nice dorado, even one dried in the sun.

Encouraged by this remark, Olivier decides to join two small hooks to make one stronger one. He joins them back to back with the end of the nylon line, which is now useless, and fixes them to the woven steel line of what was the earthing lead of the beacon. His assembly has the merit of strength, but will a fish bite at it? I cut off a tiny square of my oilskin trousers and thread it on to make a fringe which, once in the water, will make an excellent lure for these voracious fish. Olivier hesitates before throwing out his line; the problem of netting a possible catch still hasn't been solved. The rat-tail file that Alain still has in his pocket might do the trick, and with a good blow from the paddle the dorado shouldn't last long. Olivier lets his line drop without looking too sure of the effectiveness of this technique. The first one swims by without paying the least attention. The second likewise. As for the third, it stops for a moment, swims round to have a look, no doubt puzzled by the yellow lure, and goes off again without a bite. Olivier patiently tries several old fisherman's tricks. He lets out the line, then suddenly hauls it in; he gives it a few little jerks. But the quarry remains disdainful. 'Red – it's red they like. Like bulls.' Olivier isn't discouraged, and cuts out a square from the leg of his red tracksuit, hooks it on and hangs it in the place of the first lure. Well, either we've happened upon the only three blind dorado in the Atlantic, or they're not hungry, but the red doesn't attract them any more than the yellow did! I've made up my mind to have them and ask Olivier for the line. Throwing it out on my side has no better result. Alain, optimistic as ever, declares with certainty 'Relax! This evening we'll be eating spaghetti on an Italian freighter.' A chorus of four voices begs him to refrain from expressing his optimism so loudly as it brings bad luck. We all laugh at our perfectly synchronized outburst, but I thought I detected some true words in the jest. Right from the start, no sooner has Alain announced that the weather's going to improve than it's got worse. He only has to say 'Good, here's the sun' for it to disappear for the rest of the day. Or even, 'The waves aren't breaking so often' for us to get three cold showers on the trot.

The failure of this new attempt plunges us into an apathetic silence followed by a curative nap. I've noticed that as the days go by, we sleep or try to sleep more frequently. I may be unable to get to sleep during the day, but the others certainly don't deprive themselves and the frequency of discussions is proportionately less. The hours go by painfully but reassuringly slowly. Painfully, because the forced inactivity is hard to endure. But reassuringly, because every minute brings the chance of seeing another ship. This is the reason I never give up scanning the horizon. About 9 a.m. Olivier pulls my trouser leg and asks 'Hear anything?' Even cupping my ears, I can't hear anything particular among the infernal din of the breaking waves.

'Listen carefully! There's a plane flying nearby!' I assure him he must be confusing the sound of the waves, but he interrupts me: 'No, no. It's not the sound of a jet, but of a propeller!' This time I hear the regular purring: it's getting nearer. I sweep the sky with such intensity that I have the feeling that my look is piercing the thick blanket of cloud. For a moment this sound, full of a new dose of hope, seems to move away. We hold our breaths to hear it and it comes back, but still doesn't materialize in the sky. There's no plane in sight. Gliksman remarks, 'The ceiling's too low. If he's searching for us, he'll have to come down a bit.' The big word is out: 'searching'. The word everyone had on the tip of their tongue but no one dared say. This confirms our theories then: my father, or someone else, has launched a search operation. It sounds as if he's flying a bit to the north of our position: I want to shout to the pilot 'Further south, further south!' As I start worrying at still seeing nothing, Gliksman assures me that even if he's come down below the cloud cover, his search zone isn't necessarily over us. We'll probably have to wait several hours before they find us. The humming has completely disappeared now but we've more or less convinced ourselves that it *is* a search plane. Airline planes haven't had propeller engines for a long time now. Either this one or another will come back, maybe tomorrow, and find us.

It's an excellent topic of conversation to occupy our morning: how will they organize our rescue? They'll drop a new, bigger and more comfortable raft with new survival gear so that we can await the arrival of the nearest ship, which will be diverted. At any rate it's a matter of twenty-four hours, forty-eight at the most.

I've had an idea running around in my head for

several days, and with the distant passage of this plane it came back to me so strongly that I was tempted to try it. I'm still hesitating to mention it, it seems so ridiculous; I must find a method which cuts any sneering short. Five minutes later I launch into it: 'Given our situation, we could try telepathy....' Before anyone can say a word, I continue, 'No one's looking. Besides the American army has been experimenting with it. The American military have been trying this method of communication between nuclear submarine crews and their base for several years. Why don't we try?' As if I hadn't been convincing enough, I give an extra example: 'Even the Russians use telepathy, if only to win international chess tournaments. At any rate that's what their opponents claim.' My proposal arouses their curiosity, but Denis, Olivier and Alain seem to be waiting for details. 'All we have to do is to concentrate our thoughts towards someone close and communicate our last position to them, for example.' To my great relief, no one bursts out laughing, though a few reasonable remarks are accompanied by shrugs of the shoulders. I suspect they're trying out my suggestion, their eyes closed to make out they're asleep. But I've never asked them if they did, even for a minute, try to send a message by telepathy. As for me, I search among those close to me for the person most likely to be receptive to this kind of experiment. I decide on my mother. Yes *me*, who used to tease her whenever she spoke of her premonitions or her conversations with the beyond, I'm reduced to using procedures of the so-called sixth sense. For an hour, I visualize my mother in her Versailles appartment and transmit, 'Shipwrecked in the Atlantic. Last known position 36° north, 66° west – 36° north, 66° west.' I repeat these figures at the same regular rhythm as Morse code bleeps. And then, as suddenly as I started, I stop. Suppose my mother did receive my message, who would believe her? She'd just be laughed at by her friends, as usual, and my appeal would be blocked like a letter in the post when there's a strike.

After eating a quarter of a vitamin biscuit whose consistency worsens daily, turning our rations into crumbs for the birds, I get Alain to take over on lookout. I'm woken by sudden activity: Alain has just spotted the fifth ship in our lives as castaways. Still half asleep, I don't move, content to shout out at each shudder of the raft, 'Gently! Don't get so worked up. If she doesn't see us, we're going to need the "bib"!' It's strange, but this new ship doesn't interest me. I don't even want to look. Olivier, who must have been asleep too, seems to share my view. He completes my invitation to keep calm with, 'Keep cool, it won't be today.' I don't even feel the usual shaking that has accompanied the sight of a ship up till now. Judging by the comments of Gliksman, Alain and Denis, it's another tanker crossing our beam but quite far away. Once, Alain gets out a flare, but puts it down again after a few seconds. The alert didn't last long, maybe five minutes. They don't wait outside long enough for the ship to disappear. Our looks are eloquent enough not to need embroidering with words.

While bailing, Gliksman notices that the remaining flares aren't properly wrapped. Water has got into their individual little sachets. As he starts worrying about whether they'll work, Alain Gouedard hastens to reassure him. He reveals that when he was emptying the boat out to put her into the yard on the Iles des Saintes, he came across the box of flares in a sorry state and was nevertheless able to make them work. Gliksman is astonished and asks what he means. Alain smilingly recounts that to celebrate the end of the work Denis and he had a booze-up and finished with a firework display by letting off two flares! Gliksman loses his temper, screaming out, 'Like *children*! Do you imagine that I buy boxes of distress flares for you to have firework displays?' Alain and Denis weren't expecting this reaction and make no attempt to defend themselves. But Gliksman is fuming: 'What a perfectly stupid thing to do. Why didn't you let them all off? It would have been prettier!' Alain is clearly embarrassed and snaps, 'Everyone does stupid things sometimes. What's done is done.' But Gliksman is really appalled. 'It isn't just stupidity. It's ignorance. So now we have two flares less.' After thirty seconds of heavy silence, he opens his mouth as if to begin again, then changes his mind, shakes his head to express his impotence, crosses his arms and lies down on his side to try to sleep. Alain and Denis uncomfortably hand me the flares one by one after draining them and making up a plastic sleeve. The incident is forgotten when we hang up the new bag of flares, like sausages, from the canopy arch.

This is the first time Gliksman has raised his voice since the capsize, since leaving Bermuda even. He's seemed to me anxious and withdrawn since our first night in the capsule. Two days ago he began to behave like a captain again, organizing life on the raft, but not participating in it completely. Pushed up against the upright of the arch, he only moves to come and reinforce a watch. I never see him sleep for more than a quarter of an hour and he frowns like someone in deep thought whenever he closes his eyes. The lives of four boys, aged twenty-two to twenty-four, including his own son, are in his charge, and the responsibility must be crushing him. Yet all four of us try to get him to understand, by our reactions, that we assume it entirely ourselves, and that though it's natural he should be worried about his son, Alain, Olivier and I are all capable of taking care of ourselves. We in no way hold him responsible for what's happened or for what's going to happen in the hours that follow. To help us stick it out, he must stop feeling guilty. No one will blame him for this accident, whatever happens. But words alone aren't enough to lift this burden off him, so we have to go on struggling to prove to him that we're not counting on him to keep us alive.

Denis tries to find a sitting position and swears because the pain is unbearable. The slightest touch of rubber on our backsides makes us grit our teeth. Our skin is raw over our whole torsos and anywhere gripped by elastic. I decide to take drastic action and using the scissors, cut the elastic in my underpants and trouser belt in several places. The relief is truly delicious. It's like finally yawning suddenly after wanting to for several minutes. Everyone is in a sudden frenzy to cut their clothes to pieces. Within a quarter of an hour Olivier's tracksuit is reduced to rags while Denis's has become a pair of Bermuda shorts. Sighs of relief replace groans of pain. As soon as we've finished dealing with our tight waistbands, I attack the problem of water flow. Our salt water 'reserves' are situated at two main points: our trouser-leg bottoms, and our boots which act as an 'overflow'. I stab my oilskin trouser legs feverishly with the scissors. The manufacturer has used three thicknesses at this point, and the fabric resists the two blades, which pinch more than they cut. After five minutes of determination a jet of water runs out, only half emptying the little pool that I've put up with under my buttocks for two days. My jeans still hold some more and Mister Denim's cloth refuses to surrender. Finally, I pull the elastic bands out at the bottom, where the oilskin trouser legs seal over the boots. Olivier follows my example. Denis finds it difficult to make up his mind to ruin his new gear the first time he's used it, and gives up for the time being.

This evening, when Gliksman asks me what colour the sunset is, I prefer to let him admire the sight himself. The daytime star is giving way to the evening star in an explosion of red rays. A beautiful red which, according to Gliksman, means the wind should fall and the night become calm. He stays a good minute, as if to convince himself that it's not going to turn into yellow. Before slipping inside, he puts his fingers to his lips, warning me not to say anything. He too thinks we're jinxed and that we only have to mention good news for everything to get worse.

There was a seventh day and a seventh night. But this night, though slightly calmer as Gliksman had hoped, brings a frightful new spectacle. Ten minutes after the start of my watch, a thunderstorm begins. Yet the sky is clear and the stars visible for the first time. Huge flashes of light tear the celestial vault. They look as overdone as the ones in disaster films. In less than a quarter of an hour, the storm is on us. The lightning illuminates the inside of the raft through the orange canopy, tinting our faces with corpse-like colours. An incredibly violent squall of rain smashes the canvas down with the sound of a machine-gun. The shower is so heavy that within ten minutes the sea is flat and the wind has stopped. All we can hear is the deafening drumming of drops on the canopy, resonating through the whole raft. All this fresh water falling from the sky makes me thirsty. I can't reach the catchment tubes hidden behind Olivier and Gliksman, and as I can't find an empty bottle I hold one of the bailers outside. I can't leave my hand in the rain or hail for more than ten seconds: it feels like thousands of tiny freezing arrows piercing my skin. After several goes, I taste the water in the bottom of the bailer, but it's undrinkable. It's been used for bailing for seven days, is impregnated with salt and turns rainwater into brine.

When I turn in, my watch is over and the storm has moved away. But another, equally violent, arrives to surprise Olivier and Gliksman. Half asleep, I hear

Olivier shouting to make himself heard: 'Good God! The canvas is going to tear!' They can't even put their noses out for a quick look, and in any case visibility is practically nil. The whole night is punctuated with terrible showers. The floats lose a lot of pressure due to the cold and we're so frozen that reinflating them becomes a real pleasure. Each watch, the two lookouts spend twenty minutes thumping each other to get warm. The 'thumper' gets warmed up as much as the 'thumped', but by the end of the night both of them are completely exhausted and with aching arms. For the third consecutive night we're drifting southeast and no ship has crossed our path.

6

Belief and Despair

'Quick, everyone forward! We're going to sink!'
Gliksman chokes, half suffocates, his eyes bulging
and, suddenly pulling himself up, briefly upsets the
balance of the raft. His nightmare must have been
terrifying, for it takes him a good five minutes to pull
himself together. He's reassured by the just breaking
dawn, and falls asleep again. Having checked that the
sea anchor's still there, I take up my position on the
edge of the float. At seven o'clock this evening, we'll
'celebrate' the first week since being wrecked. The
compass is still showing a southeasterly drift and the
sea is getting up again, after the brief stormy calm of the
night. We still have to bail and sponge, again and again.
I've completely rubbed the skin off the base of my
fingers by pushing my hand in and out between the float
and the canopy. The little blisters which came up five
days ago have disappeared, leaving cracks caused by
seawater. I get down the signalling mirror and look at
the face of a castaway: my cheeks are hardly hollow, but
my beard accentuates the shadows and my ever wet
hair hanging down over my forehead doesn't improve

the picture. My red eyes have dark rings round them, and the skin is rough and whitened by salt. Handing the mirror to Olivier, who's asking for it, I remark, 'If you want to give yourself a fright!' We're used to one another's bedraggled faces, but discovering one's own isn't very reassuring! However, we push a lock back into place, or wipe a trail of salt off, just like vain old ladies. Without the least emotion, I notice that the anorak, hung up outside the craft the previous night, has gone. Never dry, weighed down with the litres of water it held, it was more in the way than anything else. But given that castaways never throw anything away, we were keeping it for the moment when we'd find a use for it. The distribution of the day's quarters of biscuits is no longer even accompanied by remarks. It has become a habit, and we eat them as simply as if we were having breakfast before leaving for work.

We're bored. We have no expectations of this new day, which is the best way to avoid disappointments. So that when Alain makes his usual announcement 'O.K., fellows. We'll be picked up today: this time I feel it.' We beg him to be quiet, going so far as to smilingly treat him like a jinx, which he readily admits, roaring with laughter. However, I too have a feeling that our adventure is going to be over today. I have a mental conversation with an imaginary speaker in which I explain that the situation has gone on long enough, that it's time to end this bad dream, that there's no point in keeping us waiting like this. A week is amply long enough to prove that men can survive lost at sea. Besides, there have been other demonstrations before ours, some of them even voluntary! Somewhere during the course of this dialogue I get cross with this imaginary person, blaming him for everything that's happened to us. 'Why play with our five lives? We're not ants that one pokes with a twig, or if we are, then crush us immediately with your thumb.' I end up by naming him, and addressing him as if he were a real human being: 'Why are you doing this? What do you want from us? We aren't difficult to please: all we want is for the wind to drop, the sea to calm and the sun to come out again.' Since there's no reply, I continue: 'You surely don't expect us to pray to God. We're atheists and aren't about to fall into the farce of belief.' As I follow this completely senseless internal dialogue, I tell myself that it's no more ridiculous than my idea of telepathy. As if to get rid of my mind's wanderings, I conclude, 'If it's a promise you want, O.K. you can have it!' Which is why, when a new wave fills up the raft, five minutes later, I burst out 'Good God, I swear that if we come through this, I'll go and see a rabbi.' My joke produces four gentle smiles and a remark from Alain, who exclaims while still bailing, 'I don't know if you need to see a rabbi, but if there is a god, it'd be good of him to get us out of here!'

Denis calls for quiet at the same time as me. We thought we heard the sound of a propeller plane between the explosions of two breakers. The humming seems to come from the west but the ceiling is still as low and we can see nothing. The purring of this plane is further away than the one we heard yesterday, but there's no doubt that it's there: planes are out looking for us! We listen to a first, then a second passage, until the sound of the engines gets mixed up with the waves. If he doesn't find us immediately perhaps he'll see the wreck of the trimaran, assuming that she's still afloat. If she hasn't sunk, and even if she's drifting slower than us, she still can't be very far away. But after half an hour's silence, the plane hasn't made another pass and we can't hear it anymore. It's another hard blow to our morale. If he's made a pass in our area without seeing our craft, there's little hope that he'll come back to this sector. Once again we fell into the trap of hoping too soon. The reaction to this false joy plunges us into a new period of apathy. As I assure them I can cover the 360° of the horizon from my position, they settle down to sleep.

For several days I've noticed banks of seaweed drifting north. It's slightly finer than the kind used to decorate plates of shellfish and has fruits, or rather little bladders of air, attached to flat branches. I've often thought of tasting one, but until this Monday morning had hoped that we wouldn't get to such a point. I didn't want to admit, any more than the others, that we would be on this rubber contraption for so long. Since the last packet of biscuits has been well eaten into, we need to think about some alternative source of food. The plankton net disappeared with the sea anchor, and fishing has produced no result, so there's nothing left but to try this solution. Of course, no sooner have I decided to try the seaweed than it drifts away from the raft. I make dangerous attempts to get hold of one of these yellowish clusters for half an hour and finally manage to catch one in the tips of my fingers. I have a slight qualm and search through my memory for any risks attached to eating seaweed. In the absence of any specific memory of what Bombard had to say on the subject, I pull one of the fruits off and put it in my mouth. If it makes me ill I can advise the others against trying; if not, in four days at the most we'll have to put up with it. Once the bladder has burst, there's not a lot left to chew. The skins's tough and the flesh bitter. At first taste this seaweed doesn't seem to be of much interest and I have serious doubts whether it has enough calories to be of nutritional value. I munch the little fruits for half an hour while the others are asleep or dozing. This feeding experiment has the immediate effect of making me hungry, which wasn't the effect I hoped for. Since there are no unpleasant consequences, I tell the others about my idea during the evening and suggest they have a taste. Gliksman abstains. Olivier, Denis and Alain munch this sea produce without the least sign of emotion or interest.

In the early afternoon we have another try at fishing, but it's as fruitless as the day before. So Denis suggests catching the damned dorado with a harpoon. But to harpoon, you need a harpoon! One of the paddles could be used as the shaft, but it needs a blade. One of the fresh water tins should do, if cut up and shaped. Denis and I remove the top and the bottom, using the tiny tin-opener. By folding them in two, we get two toothed semicircles which unfortunately can't be fixed to the aluminium tube of the paddle. Denis won't admit defeat and spends the rest of the day folding the tin backwards and forwards to make it give at the seam.

So the day passes, like yesterday and the day before. Most of the time is spent sleeping. Olivier sleeps the most, and when he is awake hardly speaks and doesn't seem to be interested in the groups' little jobs. He can't go ten minutes without a cold shower. Wherever he sits in the raft, he's always the first to catch a lump of water, until it becomes a bad joke. Sometimes he's the only one to be hit by an icy wave, which travels right through our shelter just to reach him. Fed up with uselessly moving about, he ends up resigned to his fate and stays put.

Two hours before sunset Alain, who's just put his head out, whispers 'Don't move, we've got company! There's a band of whales not far away.' I push down on the roof of the tent and see the enormous dorsal fins characteristic of these cetaceans about thirty metres away on the other side. Alain saw three; I can only see two and worry about what's happened to the one that's disappeared. We all know that these little eight metre whales have well-filled jaws. Gliksman reminds us that it was these same killer whales that sank the Robertson family's boat and have caused numerous other shipwrecks. It isn't known if they do it in fun or out of a taste for human flesh, but they rarely deny themselves the pleasure of overturning a hull. If they can wreck a yacht ten metres long our rubber ring won't stand up for long. Gliksman breaks the silence to declare in a quiet voice, 'I'd thought of everything, but not of ending up as a sandwich for a killer whale.' I can just see the tops of their backs in the swell, crowned with large, almost vertical fins, unlike dolphins or sharks which have slightly angled ones. Luckily they're travelling parallel to us and in the opposite direction, so they disappear rapidly enough without seeing, smelling or hearing us. I envy them their speed and their way of plunging through the waves without the least effort. But I can't take my eyes off them, terrified that they'll turn and come back to spear us. I keep on staring for a long time after they've gone, in the fear that the third one will appear at any moment. Denis and his father ask me two or three times if I can still see them, unable to hide their concern. But these charming cetaceans go on their way without showing interest in us.

Gliksman leans over the Pilot Chart once more in an effort to work out our drift and the route we've covered, producing the following theory: having capsized northwest of Bermuda, then drifted northeast for a day, southeast for a day, back northeast, and since then continuously southeast, we should, with a bit of luck, be approaching Bermuda again. What we want is for the wind to continue southerly, but above all to blow us slightly westwards. The most worrying thing is this easterly drift. If we continue to drift south we'll get into warmer and calmer waters. We've already thought of paddling if we see land. But Gliksman hastens to lessen our enthusiasm by adding that there's very little chance of happening on the coast of Bermuda and that we might miss it by miles. The idea of returning to our point of departure is sufficiently pleasant to get us imagining what our arrival would be like: after a princely departure on a superb trimaran, we would return like tramps on a rubber raft! The Bermudians' manic cleanliness wouldn't go too well with our filth and above all our stench. The indescribable smell inside the 'bib' is quite bearable, our nostrils having become used to it. But after only a few minutes, let alone a few hours, with your nose in the wind, you need another twenty minutes to get used to it again.

The sunset fires the horizon again this evening. The wind may be falling, but the night's going to be cool. For the first time, Alain admits that he's not warm and Olivier has been curled up in a corner of the raft for several hours, strangely quiet. He responds to our concern by simply saying 'I'm all right. I'm all right. I just want to sleep', which reassures us. As I've been lookout all day, everyone agrees to let me sleep all night. With no watches, I can settle down in the most sheltered corner of the 'bib', and when they change over no one will need to disturb me in order to get to the lookout position. I can fall asleep with an easy conscience and not wake up till the following morning. But a quarter of an hour later, while I'm still trying to get to sleep, a wave arrives to remind me that nowhere is completely sheltered. And I find myself bailing and sponging like the others. I manage to fall into a deep sleep between 10 p.m. and midnight, at which time a heavy shower strikes the tent, accompanied as on the previous night by lightning which shows as a violent orange light through the fabric. Gliksman tries to find the empty bottle to put the rainwater tube in, but can't for the very good reason that I'm lying on it. Undoing the gasket which seals the neck takes a good five minutes, and when we do succeed the shower stops, making us feel that everything's against us, even the weather. I finally fall asleep, determined not to move again even if I find myself up to my waist in water.

The sun, our natural alarm clock, goes off at 5.30. Olivier has settled next to me during the night. Denis has given him his slightly drier place (by 'slightly drier' must be understood 'less wet'). I go back to my favourite lookout post, taking care not to wake him. As I sit down on the float I glance automatically at the compass. It seems that our theory about getting back to Bermuda has gone completely overboard. The needle shows 30° northeast! I can't believe it, and unhook the compass to point it carefully in the direction of our drift. Gliksman, who was sleeping with one eye open, asks me if we're still headed south. I prudently reply that, unless I'm reading it wrong, the wind has turned and we're heading back north and offer him the compass to check. As he puts it down he contents himself with the hope that we won't cross the Gulf Stream whose gigantic waves would soon finish us off.

Everyone falls asleep, exhausted by their night, leaving me as sole lookout, as happens every early morning. It's the best time for deep sleep. At daylight fears disappear, the mind is freed and the muscles relax. Until about 7.30 a.m. I'm responsible for my four companions in misfortune. I sometimes glance inside and their sleep comforts me. It's as if they were saying 'You see, we trust you.' We're a single nucleus, each responsible for the others, and this is what's kept us going till this Tuesday. But how much longer must we cling to this bit of rubber? We're heading north and still drifting east. An objective assessment leads to an inevitable conclusion: we're moving further away from both land and possible shipping routes. We've only got rations for two days and the weather doesn't seem to be improving.

On the other hand it's April 17 and soon it'll be May: the weather shouldn't get worse. And also the concern in Paris and New York must have reached a peak by now. It's impossible that search and rescue operations haven't been started. Boats in our area must have been informed and their crews alerted. Also, there's a good chance that we weren't the only ones to suffer from the bad weather conditions. Finally, this is the twentieth century, and in the twentieth century people don't die as castaways. If we'd been able to 'stay put', it'd all be over by now.

Denis has just sat down and unwrapped his pieces of tin. Last night he was careful to wind them up in strips of plastic bag, to be sure not to puncture the raft. He folds and refolds them, still half asleep, convinced that they'll give in the end and, once shaped, will become effective weapons to catch and kill our dorado companions. As Alain begins to open his eyes I exchange a scheming look with Denis, and before he can say a thing Denis gags him with a hand, saying, 'Don't say a thing!' to which I add eagerly: 'No boat today, no shower tonight, no coffee or spaghetti, don't say a thing, not a thing!' Alain is taken aback but smilingly asks permission to say 'Good morning' and having received it, continues 'Good, well then, good morning everyone!'

An hour later Gliksman hands out our rations, which we wash down with two turns of water. We're a lot thirstier than yesterday, in fact. Even without heat, we're beginning to dehydrate. This leads to a debate on the need to drink a little seawater as a provision for more difficult times. After half an hour's discussion we still can't decide. Some say that if you get used to it a little at a time, it's not dangerous; others, with me among them, have doubts, believing that science hasn't yet recognized this theory developed by Alain Bombard. To fill the long lethargic silence that follows this debate, Denis tells us about a frustrating dream he's had for two nights. It's always the same situation. He's spending the morning with his mother and his friends, but when the time for lunch arrives he leaves them at the entrance to a restaurant, saying 'Sorry I can't have lunch with you, but at the moment I'm on a liferaft adrift in the middle of the Atlantic', and he wakes up to find that his dream is a reality.

Today seems longer to me than previous days. Bailing and sponging become routine tasks, and although some people never get tired of looking at the sea from a Mediterranean beach we're no longer among them. Every wave has the same hostile look to us, the clouds are no more than vulgar barometers which won't indicate fine weather, and the sun's appearances are so brief that you can count them on your fingers. What would be good would be to see a coastline, a ship or a plane. The only distraction this Tuesday morning is the brief passage of a little starling-like bird, which makes me hope for a moment that we might be near land. I know that dozens of species of birds venture very far and that seeing them doesn't at all mean that land is near, but it makes me feel good to think that the bird flying over our craft isn't one of them. Denis is still struggling with his tins; he's got cramps in his hands from twisting them back and forth, but they won't give. As the dorado are still circling the raft, we ask Olivier to have another go at fishing. When he doesn't reply, we shake him hard, but he grumbles that he wants to sleep some more and has no intention of fishing. Gliksman has to gently reprimand him, suggesting that he pulls himself together. But Olivier seems to have difficulty raising himself up and sitting down. We again ask him if he feels all right. As he unrolls the fishing line, he says: 'No problems, it's just that I feel really sleepy.' Gliksman discreetly asks us if Olivier often behaved like this when we were on board *RTL-Timex*, but none of us had noticed this power of sleep before. Slouched across the float, his arm hanging carelessly in the water, Olivier is obviously trying hard not to fall asleep again. I suggest replacing him for fear that he might let the line go. Speaking with difficulty, he admits that it might be best. Gliksman is alerted by this speech difficulty and tries to find out what is weakening Olivier.

'Are you hurting anywhere? Are you cold?' He explains in the same painful manner that actually he isn't very warm but feels an overwhelming need to sleep. So we have to try to get him to accept the woollen pullover that Gliksman takes off and hands him. In the end it's Alain Gouedard who has the last word: 'Don't be an idiot, Olly, it's going to be a cold night and if you're cold now, you won't make it.' We discover that all he's got on, underneath his oilskins, is a wet anorak and a light cotton shirt! So for nine days he must have been dying of cold and said nothing. Furthermore, he was barefoot the first four days and this must have lead to a great loss of heat. He's never recovered physically from his exhaustion from nearly drowning at the time of the capsize. And what about the red stain he thought he saw around the wreck? It couldn't have been from my slight head wound and there was no red liquid on board. He must have hit his head and a moment's unconsciousness disturbed his sight.

Night's beginning to come on and my fishing watch has produced nothing. I decide to leave the line in the water. Maybe there'll be a fish on it tomorrow. Before organizing ourselves for the night, Denis suggests that we swallow half a glucose tablet to help us fight the cold. The cold's been increasing for forty-eight hours and the permanently stagnating water in the bottom of the 'bib' is no longer even warmed by our bodies. Having eaten our tablets, we huddle up together for the night, the ninth since we were wrecked. This evening, Alain doesn't suggest himself for the first watch, but hastens to curl up in a corner to sleep. He doesn't risk his usual optimistic remark, doubtlessly remembering our morning warning. Gliksman repeats his call for vigilance, advising us to look round the horizon at least every quarter of an hour. It's too cold to keep our faces outside continuously. In placing myself against the base of the canopy arch I accidentally get caught in the little ring round one of the decompression valves for the float, luckily without pulling it out, but I'm concerned at the thought that a bad dream might lead me to pull on this ring, which becomes as obsessive as the alarm cord in a train is for the person who's sleeping in the top bunk.

This third starry night isn't only cold in temperature, but looks cold. Visibility is perfect. The waves are breaking cleanly but the rollers vanish quickly. Tiny phosphorescent particles stick to the float for a few seconds. The wind stings my face and its noise still discomforts me. The exploding of the waves gets more powerful during the night, like an attack by a virtual squadron of fighters. Another storm breaks over us about 11 p.m. Gliksman has taken precautions tonight and slips the rainwater tube into the bottle. In less than ten minutes it's full of fresh water, which Gliksman is anxious to taste and offers around, saying that it's 'delicious'. It's a treat – no taste of the plastic or rust which we've got used to, and cold as if it had come from a refrigerator. Olivier refuses to drink, but the four of us finish the litre. But the shower hasn't stopped and Gliksman continues collecting, transferring the contents of the bottle to the jerry cans every ten minutes. The second advantage of this violent rain is that it calms the sea by flattening the waves. Which doesn't stop one pouring into the 'bib', shocking us it's so cold. Olivier didn't budge a bit; he didn't even complain, and

Alain simply changes position. Without stopping our bailing and sponging, we're really worried about this turn of events.

Olivier is allowing himself to be completely taken over by the false peace of the numbness due to cold and Alain is going the same way. The three of us force them to sit up. Denis and I start rubbing them energetically and thumping their backs. Gliksman tries to repair the little interior light, which is going on and off in the swell. Denis suggests that we should again take glucose, doubling up Olivier's and Alain's ration. Gliksman hesitates and Alain lets drop, 'We've got to the point where we might as well finish the rations to last one more night.' I put on my hardest voice to try and get Olivier to react: 'For goodness sake, Olivier, stir yourself, don't let go: if you give up, we've all had it! You've no right to let yourself die!' But his only reply is an incomprehensible grunt. Gliksman forces half a glucose tablet into his mouth and gives another to Alain. Denis, who's been amazingly clear-thinking and active, suggests that we should warm them up by arranging ourselves like a sandwich. As Gliksman moves the two jerry cans he notices that they're splitting; the plastic has been deformed by our sitting on them and long creases have appeared on the sides. Nevertheless, we put them in the bottom of the 'bib' so that Alain can lie on them, isolated from the water. Taking care not to upset the craft, we lay Olivier on top of Alain and Denis gets down on his knees and presses his torso against Olivier. The night's getting colder and colder and I too am starting to shiver. Denis asks me if I can try and warm up Alain's and Olivier's feet. I try breathing on them through the wool of their socks and then rubbing them and holding them against my skin, opening my clothes to do it. To stop this human bundle from falling over, I block their legs with my knees and grip their feet in my arms. Gliksman watches us without flinching and leaves it to us to work it out. I have the impression that he's withdrawn from the game. He knows perfectly well what this general weakening means and what its consequences will be.... As if deciding to know the worst, he seizes Olivier's wrist and takes his pulse, using his watch. He says nothing when he lets go, so Denis says, 'Well...?' After three seconds' hesitation, his father murmurs, 'Fifty, hardly fifty beats a minute.'

7

The Most Beautiful Ship in the World

The pain is too great. I must change position. Olivier's and Alain's bodies have slipped slightly since we arranged them. Their feet are crushing my belly and I'm finding it harder and harder to breathe. But if I try to push them back, they'll wake up and we'll have to start from the beginning again. I must hang on, I must hang on...I can hardly turn my head to look outside. To look at what, anyway? I can barely see 20° either way.

The cold has never been so keen. I feel as if I'm sitting on an iceberg, the night is so freezing. Until tonight I've put up with a little pool of water round me, but now it's become unbearable and I must find the sponge and finally dry it up. The water's so cold it hardens my flesh and I feel as if my buttocks were like marble. If the pain didn't grip me so hard I could sleep. Why not? It won't be long now, since after Olivier it will be Alain's turn, and then? Maybe mine, or Denis's, or his father's. But if this temperature lasts till the following night, and perhaps the one after that, well, there's no point in deluding ourselves: we may well have thought we were saving our lives by getting into this thing, but we now must fear that it has condemned us to a slow death.

Then there's this unbearable pain in my belly. Alain's just slipped off the jerry can and his feet are digging deeper into my stomach. He has to rearrange himself, and we must redo the whole group, which means I can breathe for a bit while we reorganize. Gliksman takes advantage of this to ask me to warm him up by thumping him on his back – 'Harder! Harder!' – even though I feel as if I'm hitting him like a brute, using all the energy I've got left. It feels as if I've got no arms left and as I'm half twisted, I'm afraid I might strain my kidneys.

Taking advantage of this relative ease, I part the flaps to look out, more out of habit than conviction. When I go to close them, the rubber toggle comes off in my hand. The glue's given way. The last straw is that the light's just gone out. Using my nails and teeth, I try to pierce the canvas in the dark to push a bit of elastic through like a buttonhole. I go at it with such force that instead of a small buttonhole I make a long tear that threatens to get bigger with each gust of wind. Without being too aware of what I've botched up, I manage to get the two flaps closed. From now on it will be virtually impossible to use this opening to look out. If I contort myself unbelievably and risk straining my neck, I can just manage to see a tiny bit of sky and a few square metres of water, which amounts to seeing nothing any more.

Olivier hasn't stirred during the whole regrouping operation, but there's absolutely nothing we can do except wait till morning. In this cold, with no light, there's no way we can try to revive him. But what could we try, in fact? And in the end I'm sure I envy him for he's fading away without knowing it, his relaxed face evidence of the gentleness of his departure.

But what decision will we have to take tomorrow? It's no good hiding from reality. We'll have a corpse in the raft with us, perhaps two if Alain doesn't manage to revive either. In order to 'stick it out' will we have to throw it into the water, to throw *them* into the water? In order still to 'stick it out' will we have to take their clothes off before throwing them into the water? I just can't believe it will come to such a pass. For the moment I won't admit the possibility. But tomorrow, or the day after, if I'm confronted with such a situation how will I react? In other times and places men have shown themselves capable of what no animal would do in order to survive. In the end wouldn't it be best for us all to die together?

I try to resist sleep, but feel drowsiness taking me over, and can't struggle against it. It must be 2.30 a.m. when I close my eyes, not without a last look at my tiny bit of sky and two or three waves.

It's 3 o'clock. Alain Gliksman is alone on watch. He's containing his rage, obsessed with the idea of leaving a message, with the idea of leaving some evidence of our journey on this liferaft. It would be too easy for us to be 'lost at sea' with no further explanation. We didn't die, drowned near the trimaran, but for nearly ten days we've survived and hoped, and Gliksman wants to find a shock-phrase that will explain everything in three words. It would be too laborious to describe our whole trip and besides we haven't got the materials we'd need to do it. However, a single phrase, written across Denis's passport for example, would suffice. Something like: 'We're dying, victims of appalling equipment.' While busily concocting the details of this tirade he looks out over the surface of the water as a matter of form; to the right, nothing... straight ahead, nothing... to the left....

It's 3.05 and I'm torn out of my sleep by Alain Gliksman's shout of 'A ship, a ship!' Denis has leapt up and we're both preparing to calm him and help him out of his dream, but he's shouting still louder: 'Quick, a ship, she's enormous!'

Without giving us time to get up, Gliksman adds in a blank, choking voice, 'She's coming straight for us! The fool's going to sink us!' Before he can even finish his sentence, a huge freezing wave strikes the craft and half fills it with water, waking us up completely. Alain Gouedard, who has totally pulled himself together, flings himself on the flare bag, shouting 'The knife, the knife!' I grope feebly around me but Denis, who'd kept it in his pocket, is already handing it to Alain who attacks the thick plastic sack suspended from the tent arch. He takes the first tube that comes to hand and tearing the fabric to get it out quicker, kneels down on the float and pulls the firing cord. Unfortunately, we've got out a red hand flare by mistake, not a rocket. Now we're skirting the immense steel wall, a good dozen metres in height; we're so close we can feel the vibrations and hear her engines.

We can't believe that the duty officer can see us from the bridge, for even the red light of the hand flare must be hidden by the hull. Alain throws it up into the air in his agitation, without our being able even to see where it falls. In the general excitement I must have torn the canopy where I made the repair two hours earlier, and Denis and I jostle in the opening. Standing next to Alain, Gliksman suddenly starts shouting 'Help!' He's lost his voice but he puts his hands round his mouth at the risk of falling and shouts louder. It's awful. I've never in my life heard such a despairing cry, yet paradoxically, it's tremulous with hope. His howling is infectious and now we're all shouting at once except Olivier, who still hasn't realized the crucial nature of the situation. Denis is shouting himself hoarse like a cracked record – 'Help! Help!' – stuck on the vowel. For his part, Alain shouts till he's breathless, while getting another flare out. As for me, I'm whistling fit to bust, with two fingers in my mouth. The rocket was upside down and fires straight into the water.

She's going away.

Now we can see the white light indicating her stern. It's impossible! She hasn't seen us! Still we keep up our hullaballoo and Gliksman hands another tube to Alain, taking care to give it the right way up this time. The rocket climbs, printing a long red trail. Denis stops shouting and, pulling on our trouser legs, asks for silence: 'The engines have changed their note! She's turning!' Alain waits for a while before letting off the next rocket flare. I'm clenching my teeth and fists; I'm extremely tense, holding my breath, and my temples are throbbing enough to burst my head. Alain can't wait any longer to launch the fourth flare, which climbs as high into the sky as the previous one. Olivier's sitting up but still hasn't made up his mind to look outside.

The ship does seem to have slowed down, but I can't bear to look at her any more, without knowing why, and I get back in and sit down. Olivier finally deigns to investigate the cause of all this hoo-hah, and sticks his head out. Gliksman remarks, breathlessly, 'Her green light's gone out... no, it's disappeared... wait, I think she's turning!' With my hands clenched on my cheeks I claw my face, softly repeating, half crying, 'Let them have seen us! Let them have seen us!' Gliksman's still not sure: 'She's beam-on... she's a tanker. She's turning! She's turned! That's it, I can see two white lights! She's coming back, she's coming back to look for us!' Alain's just lit a hand flare: he lifts it up over his head as if to dislocate his arms. He looks like the Statue of Liberty, and what liberty!

This time our cries are cries of joy, accompanied by nervous laughter. We'd certainly jump up and down, if the raft would let us. We're mad, exultant: 'She's seen us! She's seen us! It's all over!' It wouldn't take much for us to kiss one another. I don't know if I'm crying or laughing or both at once. It's the most beautiful thing I've ever seen. She's the most beautiful ship in the world. The bridge and gangway lights are repeated in the portholes and the water. She looks like a floating crystal palace. We can't stop laughing. Gliksman gasps, 'To think she nearly sank us, that fool!' Denis comments on her manoeuvre: 'Superb! She's going to stop abeam and protect us from the wind and swell!' The sound of her engines fills our ears and smothers us in happiness. A slight smell of fuel begins to drift towards us. Someone's turned on a spotlight and is sweeping the waves with its beam, without pointing at us however.

Alain announces that he's just about to light the last hand flare, but for some reason Gliksman wants to keep it. Alain didn't wait for the go-ahead and has lit it. Immediately the spotlight beam is pointed at us. We're about 200 metres away on her starboard side and can just make out running shadows on the bridge. As we don't see the shape of a launch about to be lowered, Alain and Denis begin paddling. In all the excitement, we've forgotten to haul in the sea anchor, so the first few strokes of the paddles are more or less useless. We get rid of this brake, but then Alain's and Denis's unco-ordinated movements result in making the 'bib' spin on its axis. Furthermore, the sea's still as rough and it takes at least six strokes of the paddles to advance a single metre. Slowly but surely we draw near to the tanker. We can see about twenty crew members from this distance, leaning against the bulwarks. Now we're obsessed to know what nationality they are. We get our sense of humour back, leading to a few remarks such as: 'I hope they're not Russians, or we'll find ourselves in Cuba', or even 'I think I saw a Belgian. Better go back, it's too risky!' The nearer we get the more feverishly excited the tanker's crew gets, shouting then clapping to encourage us. We're scarcely twenty metres away, but the current is carrying us towards the stern. Denis panics, afraid that we'll get caught up in the turbulence from the propellers. But the duty officer, who's already demonstrated his manoeuvring skill, puts her into reverse and distances us sufficiently from the turbulence. Alain is redoubling his effort, while Denis is weakening, and the 'bib' begins spinning again. By the time they've found their rhythm we're 200 metres away again. I get the last two glucose tablets out and forcibly stoke up the mouths of the two rowers, who spit half of it out. Denis loses patience because he's got his paddle caught up in the fishing line I deliberately left out yesterday evening. He's running out of energy and breaks the rhythm. After strongly resisting my attempt to relieve him, he finally accepts and hands me the paddle.

The tanker crew is still encouraging us with a sort of 'Heave ho!' Gliksman waves to them and remarks to Alain, 'Can you imagine what would have happened if that first flare, which you certainly threw up on deck, had made her explode and we'd found ourselves in *two* liferafts throwing stones at each other?'

This time we manage to approach the tanker's hull and grab the two hawsers thrown to us. The swell lifts us up and down the tanker's sides, as high as three-quarters of the way up her freeboard. Two sailors throw down a rope ladder which Olivier tries to grab, while Alain and I hang onto the hawsers with all our might. Olivier stands on the float, gets hold of the side ropes and finally manages to get one foot on the bottom rung, only to find himself perched on this tiny step, five metres below the level of the 'bib' owing to the movement of the swell and the rolling of the ship. Half an hour ago he couldn't move his little finger, but now he's climbing like a goat in an assault on the tanker, welcomed by *'Bravo!'* and the shouts of joy of her crew. Then it's Denis's turn, who gets up to the deck with no problems. Meanwhile Gliksman has been gathering up the contents of the 'bib', shoving the bailers, compass, sponges, first-aid kit wholesale into the canvas bag.

Now it's my turn to stand on the float and place a foot on a rung halfway up the rope ladder. What an extraordinary feeling: I'm actually standing up for the first time in nine long days! I wait for Gliksman to hand me the bag from the raft, which is going up and down like a lift. I catch the bag as it practically flies past on its third vertical journey. It makes climbing the ladder difficult. Above I can make out the crew who are gesturing to me to let it drop, for it must weigh about seven kilos. I take it between my teeth – it's like biting a feather pillow – and attack the climb. At the top I'm gripped by hands which swing me over the bulwarks and then help me up. I make them understand that I can stand, only to find that my legs have become jelly, the deck gives way and I collapse in a burst of laughter. So two sailors grasp me and drag me along without letting me take a single step, while asking me at every turn 'O.K.? O.K.?' to which I can only reply stupidly: 'O.K.!'

They take me to the galley where I find Denis waiting, hilariously leaning against a stove. Our rescuers are Italian and try to make themselves understood in a mixture of Italian and rough French and English, all joined together with grand gestures. They suggest changing our wet clothes for blankets which we accept without a fuss. I'm afraid of dirtying their galley when I take my oilskin trousers off, convinced that there's twenty litres of water in each leg. In fact there's only a litre in each boot, but I'll never forget the feeling.

Olivier's just rejoined us. As he was the first on board, two sailors wanted to take him up to the bridge immediately to meet the second in command, out of respect for the rules of hospitality. But they had to give up their idea on the way, since the goal of their trip was three levels higher and Olivier couldn't get past the first. Alain is next to be deposited in the same way, followed by Gliksman who left the raft after his crew more to personally ensure the loading of our 'bib' than for thoughts of traditions of the sea, because he hasn't given up his idea of exhibiting the thing at the next Paris Boat Show.

What a wonderful feeling, to take off all our clothes and wrap ourselves up in dry woollen blankets. And you can't imagine the joy of sitting in a deep, soft sofa. The crew settle us down in the officers' messroom for a virtual press conference, for our rescuers want to know everything: where we're from, what happened to us, who we are and how long we'd been drifting in our rubber raft. To return their politeness I try to speak Italian, using the few words I know plus a lot of others that I invent by adding an I, an A, or an O to French words. This charms them and convinces them that I can speak their language fluently, so they launch into a veritable speech in which the word '*miracolo*' occurs incredibly often. The coffee flows like water into cups which already have whisky in them. This method of sudden feeding doesn't seem a good idea, but how can we refuse? The only offer to be refused, with lively cries of disgust, is a big plate of biscuits!

Overcome, pampered, our thirst quenched, we don't know how to thank them; we can't speak any more, our muscles relax, our heads are buzzing, our skin stinging. We still can't quite realize what's happened. Our replies to their questions are short: trimaran – nine days – vitamin biscuits – tempest – capsized.... We're simultaneously drunk with well-being, questions, fatigue, and possibly also whisky. Alain finds a way to say Thank You. He takes his wristwatch off and gives it to the nearest sailor. We follow his example. They're all we have left, but we offer them with sincere happiness.

Meanwhile the Captain's been woken up, together with the Chief Engineer, and we see them come in with their respective wives. He introduces himself in French, enhanced with a delightful Italian accent: 'Captain Giovanni Busetto. Welcome on board the *Afran Dawn*. The *Afran Dawn* is a Liberian tanker of 120,000 tons, transporting an American cargo with an Italian crew. She's just loaded crude oil in Angola and is on her way to Philadelphia, which means another three days at sea – plenty of time to recover.

After reassuring Captain Busetto with '*Tutto va bene!*' a few times, and having our photos taken, we can finally put the question we're all dying to ask:'Have you been warned to keep a lookout for us?' The reply cuts like a knife: '*Niente de niente!*' No search operation has even been started. The planes we heard were just passing, without even looking at the water. After giving our parents' particulars so that the radio operator can pass on the news, we're conducted to our quarters by the Captain himself. Our walk through the gangways and companionways could easily be misinterpreted as the swayings of five alcoholics.

Gliksman finds himself in an individual cabin, while we're put in the sick-bay. Here at last are the dry sheets we've dreamed of day and night. Yet we're unable to appreciate them right away because we toss and turn for two hours, unable to benefit from the reclining position. Our wounds find this contact with soft, cool, cloth difficult. We have to keep reminding ourselves that it's not a dream!

At 6 o'clock in the morning, the officers' steward brings us cheese sandwiches and a cup of tea. At last we have warmth, space, taste... all that's missing is a hot shower. But I have the feeling that on the *Afran Dawn* you only have to wish for it to come true. The shower is in the room next to the sick-bay and Olivier, yesterday's near-corpse, is the first to partake of this new pleasure. We can hear his groans of pleasure and satisfied swearing through the wall. He's hardly out before I'm tearing in to take his place. I feel strangely apprehensive before turning on the hot tap: I've been soaked to the skin for nine days, and now that I'm dry I've only got one idea in my head, and that's to get wet again. After a second's hesitation, I plunge in. Warm water runs like rain over my poor skin, wiping away burns, aches, and finally relaxing me. I could stay under this warm torrent for hours, but the others are waiting their turn, and I'm not going to become selfish after nine days of communal life at close quarters!

Lunch follows another period of rest: spaghetti, mountains of spaghetti. And it goes on for three days... three days in which we are the children of the Captain and crew of the *Afran Dawn*. The tanker's ours. Giovanni Busetto offers her, as does the cook, the engineer, the painter, the steward; one a pair of socks, another his shirt, another his jacket, his razor, his trousers.

For this big Italian family our recovery has been no less than a miracle: the previous Sunday, they had to replace a piston and the boat drifted north: *on Wednesday at 3.05 a.m. the Afran Dawn was twenty miles off course.* When Alain Gouedard hears this, in the middle of the city of the engineroom, this self-proclaimed atheist, optimist, disbeliever admits, 'I've never had a mystical thought in my life, but it makes me wonder.' Giovanni Busetto, Peppone as we've nicknamed him, has to withdraw discreetly with tears in his eyes.

Half an hour before we disembark the sailors all want us to autograph their tee-shirts. We're more than miracles for them, we're 'stars'! Our situation is embarrassing to say the least. When we got our things back from the ship's laundry we found the only treasure left from the wreck was a half-dissolved 100 franc note. We all sign it and hand it over to Signor and Signora Busetto, declaring in our best Italian that the *Afran Dawn* will always be *'la più bella barca del mondo'* [the most beautiful ship in the world] for us.

Later, there'll be Norman Lemieux, a Boeing 747 nearly missed in New York, and the reunions at Roissy Airport. There'll also be tears, laughs, joy, fatigue, microphones, photographs...

'I didn't die because I had such a lot left to say.'
—Michel Polnareff

8

Tears of Reunion

On April 18, 1980, in a liferaft moored at the foot of the Pont de l'Alma on the Seine in Paris, we'll blow out our first birthday candle. There'll be two jerry cans of champagne and three packets of biscuits. Our civilian status will have changed, even if the civil administration doesn't realize it: Alain Gliksman, Denis Gliksman, Olivier Redkine, Alain Gouedard and Nicolas Angel, born April 18, 1979 at 3.05 a.m. on board the Liberian tanker *Afran Dawn*. Having had the option of a first try at a lifestyle, it seems to us that it would be interesting to change its makeup in order to appreciate a second. For example, we can't help smiling at the little worries of daily life. I've forgotten the times when the arrival of the demand for a third of the year's income tax would keep me from sleeping, when I used to lose my temper in traffic jams, or I was irritable because it was raining. How ridiculous my reactions seem to me now! How could I have thought such insignificant things important? I must shamefully admit today that I had no knowledge of the value of things. Doubtless I lacked the factors for comparison of one event with another.

From now on I have this reference point – we all have. At Kennedy Airport in New York, Alain made a remark that revealed our new way of dealing with life. As we'd arrived too late to check in and hadn't any money, we were preparing to spend the night in the airport terminal. We didn't like this new episode, but all it took was 'It'll be better than the raft' to make our worrying seem derisory and to make us laugh at this new episode in our adventures. Furthermore, we didn't miss the plane.

Before getting into that rubber ring we were five, defined by our five different personalities, five different minds, five ways of thinking. Then for nine days we were only 'one'. Then we were an entity that was trying not to self-destruct, by constantly keeping up its morale and its will to live. If one of us let go, the group's unity would be broken and our chances of 'sticking it out' would fade. Right from the first day we knew that we mustn't break. If one of us gave up, it would affect the others' morale and might drag them down too. We had to stay calm: not to show off, for we had nothing left to prove, but for the sake of our companions in misfortune. We had to keep hoping, or at the very least *pretend* that we were, to the others. So everyone struggled in his own way, according to his personality.

My natural tendency to clear-thinking pessimism was contrasted to Alain Gouedard's unshakeable optimism. I've already said that Alain's bursts of laughter, his visions of hope, his strong character which helped him to face anything, sustained us all from start to finish. I never detected the slightest trace of despair in his attitude whatever the circumstances. Yet he too thought we were lost. During the last twenty-four hours he too had his journey through the desert. He admitted to me, a week after our rescue, that in another few hours

the *Afran Dawn* would only have picked up four castaways. He was weakening and he knew it. He knew he'd
be second on the final list. He'd made a decision to go
overboard while he still had the strength to do it. He
couldn't bear the idea of being watched as he died. He'd
also been forced by cool, thoughtful reckoning to arrive
at the more important conclusion that Denis, Alain
Gliksman and I would stand a better chance with the
disappearance of two near-corpses. Without wishing to
sound pretentious, I think the expression 'spirit of sacri-
fice' is the one to employ to describe this type of
situation.

Olivier sealed himself into a prudent silence,
covering his anguish with a mask of indifference.
Nothing seemed to impress him. He never or rarely
launched into optimistic fantasies, as the four of us did.
When a ship passed he acted like us to help our recovery, but as soon as she was no more than a tiny dark
spot on the horizon Olivier was content to listen to our
talk without joining in. He was doubtless weakened
during the capsize and never fully recovered, allowing
himself to sink into the pleasant lethargy induced by
cold. Already for twenty-four, if not forty-eight, hours
Olivier had been sinking gently into a sleep from which
he'd never wake. But he smiled in this sleep and his
smile reassured us. Yet death from exposure is an insi-
dious end, gentle and without suffering, for by the time
it's been diagnosed it's already almost too late.

Denis was without doubt the least able among us to
hide his concern. He couldn't hide his fear when faced
with the violence of the waves and hung on to the hope
that we'd encounter a ship. Whenever we had to admit
that a ship hadn't seen us, he protested energetically at
our, in his view, too quick resignation. Activity was his
facade. He spent the night in the survival capsule
judging the water level and trying to close the exit

hatch. In the 'bib' he rigged up a lure and a harpoon blade, and when the idea of approaching death began to come into our minds during the last night he busied himself mending the light or arranging Olivier's position. Denis would not accept that two members of the same family could disappear at the same time. He hung on to the image of his mother, believing that he and his father had no right to leave her in such a way without warning.

Alain Gliksman himself struggled by reasoning, analysing, calculating, weighing our chances, but as the man who had the ultimate responsibility. He was the skipper, the oldest and the most knowledgeable in matters of sailing, if not in survival. Alain's authority was never questioned, though he never needed to use it. We could all four of us have been his sons, a thought that was itself enough to make him feel guilty, and nothing ever lead us to believe that Denis was more especially so than us. As I've already said two or three times, there was no favouritism on board and the apparent indifference between father and son even caused a certain amount of discomfort among the rest of us. Then, Alain was a prisoner of his own reputation as a good sound sailor and he feared that this was the reason for the late arrival of help, and thereby for our loss. He thought and said (and he was absolutely right) that no one would worry about the 'careful Gliksman'. After all, he'd declared to the journalists of the yachting press before the departure for the Route de Rhum race: 'I chose *Three Legs of Mann II* [the original name of *RTL-Timex*] because she's one of the safest trimarans ever built. I know that with her, I won't get tossed like a pancake.' He was angry with himself for having believed that 'accidents only happen to other people'. After three days in the raft his attitude changed: he obviously thought we'd be picked up within three days. On Tuesday and even on Wednesday, he himself started discussions on subjects that might make us relax. He was the one who tried to organize party games, who laughed uncontrollably at my descriptions of certain famous media personalities. And then, from one day to the next, his face changed. His mask reappeared. He spent hours analysing and reanalysing the reasons for our capsize. He worked out our drift, he tried to forecast the weather by observing the shape of the clouds, the troughs of waves or the colour of the sunset. Sometimes he seemed to want to convince himself as to the validity of his catch-phrase 'We must stick it out.' He underlined it with specific detail: 'If we're to stick it out, we absolutely must not allow ourselves to succumb to despair. People have been known to die of cold locked in cold stores that weren't even working.' But he developed all his demonstrations with scientific rigour, leaving nothing to chance. His latest attitude which permitted him to withdraw into himself seemed obvious even when he forced himself to sleep. Crouching down, his forehead creased, Alain was still thinking and calculating. When he wasn't analysing the present situation, he was building future plans. He never stopped conceiving of improvements to *RTL-Timex*, if she was picked up, or to future trimarans. Even if they couldn't be prevented from overturning, it should at least be possible to make them absolutely unsinkable. He kept flying into a rage when discussing the raft's manufacturer. But his projects for the future were never preceded with the word 'if'.

In fact, no one used this 'if'. We never said 'If we get out of this, the builder will hear a thing or two!' On the contrary, we expressed affirmation, not to say certainty: 'The builder *will* hear a thing or two!' Obviously for the others as much as for me, the 'if' was there in our minds, but to have said it would have revealed a kind of despair. So we couldn't show signs of the slightest feelings of this kind without risking destroying the group's solidarity. A solitary castaway must sorely miss the enormous moral support that such a group gives. He'd certainly be more vulnerable, more easily discouraged, which would lead him ultimately to death by resignation. We were aware of this, and it sometimes happened that we talked of Alain Colas, but we would change the subject very quickly, doubtless out of a sense of decency. However, there were never any moments of common despair, and this was due I think to the 'good behaviour' of the group. In the end everyone had his bad patch, but the others were there, able to come to his aid if needed, and with the exception of Olivier on the last night it never came to that.

The physical closeness, which reminded us of the delights of the Paris *Métro* during the rush-hour, was also, as I said, a lesson in self-control. It made us extremely and artificially polite to one another. This politeness was one of the guarantees of understanding within the group. If everyone had allowed himself to swear or make unpleasant remarks each time he was disturbed by his neighbour, the atmosphere would certainly have deteriorated and might have lead to a bitterness that time wouldn't have been able to erase. We had plenty of targets for our bad temper just in the subjects of the raft, the sea, the gales or blind ships.

At night our dreams were also a kind of release; unfortunately their content was always related to the reality of the moment. Gliksman and I thought we'd seen ships; we were so sure of it that we cried out, causing general panic on board. As for Alain 2, he was still aboard the trimaran, but with badly set sails, locked hatches between the cabins, and lost cabin keys.

Denis's dream always began with a pleasant situation, usually in Paris, but ended with him gaining consciousness and saying, still dreaming, 'No, it's impossible, I can't do that, I'm on a liferaft in the middle of the Atlantic at the moment.' Olivier kept his silence even while asleep and was the only one not to talk in his sleep or tell us about his dreams. Once rescued, either on the ship or back in France, we stopped dreaming or at any rate we couldn't remember having dreamed on waking. Above all, we felt we wanted to forget what our life was like during those difficult days, and we refused to relive them even in our thoughts.

However, certain events will always remind us of those nights and days. Thus, one evening on a Mediterranean beach I had the curious sensation of feeling my stomach turn over when I heard the waves breaking on the rocks, the way it did when a wave of the 'jet-plane' type struck our craft. This traumatic noise is certainly the strongest memory of our experience. Just talking about it brings the sound back into my memory. This noise isn't the only thing to have a land equivalent, but the suction too. The violence of the waves' striking was always preceded by a depressive effect which caused a whirlwind. This suction was not very different from what happens when a lorry tears past at high speed on a highway. In fact, a couple of times Denis had warned of the impending arrival of waves by shouting 'Watch out! We're being overtaken by a 15-tonner!' We often talk about these feelings when we're together, as we often talk about our dreams because, once over, they seem almost comic to our eyes.

On the other hand there are personal areas which we don't admit to and which have a certain form of mysticism. So can I put forward the idea that we all thought of God, or of some supreme force of divine origin? Well I don't see why I should be the only one of the five of us to have felt a state of half-belief during our journey, when I don't usually see things in this light, for I was no more likely than them to go and pray in a church, a temple or a synagogue. I had no more cause than them to hang onto an image of God. Furthermore, I'd also often been exasperated by the spectacle of a religious service. All of which proves that we were, and still are, five convinced atheists. Yet behind these closed doors, phrases or scraps of phrases revealed everyone's mystical thoughts, even if they were unconscious.

A particular question that demands explanation was Alain Gliksman's obsessional 'What have we done to deserve such punishment?' If we felt this so strongly, it was because our appalling situation seemed to us undeniably willed by a superior being who was playing with us. Right up to the last moment, everything seemed to prove to us that we were pathetic actors in a kind of sadistic game: atmospheric conditions forced us to struggle to the limit of our strength, and then just when we felt we couldn't go on, a semblance of calm weather would arrive to give us the minimum possible time to get our breath back, and when we'd recovered the gale would start up again even stronger. It all seemed to happen as if a hand pushed our heads under water and at the precise moment when we were drowning the hand let go, only to begin again five seconds later. It really seemed like an infernal cycle, followed like a routine, and from capsize to rescue it never let up: the joy of finding Olivier alive was followed by the threat of sinking with the wreck of the trimaran. The relief of having embarked in the liferaft was followed by its capsize. And while this little game continued, everything seemed to happen as if to make us understand that we could never stop struggling to stay alive.

Finally, we came to the last night and the end of all our illusions, for Olivier was lost and with the persisting bad weather a delay of forty-eight hours would have got the better of our resistance. There was only one possibility of rescue left for us: encountering a ship in our path. And that's exactly what happened, with such a wealth of coincidences that one really must ask a certain number of questions. To be saved, we benefitted from a chance in a million, a miracle, a Liberian ship that was crossing outside the normal shipping lanes. What about those twenty miles off course, thanks to which our paths crossed with the precision of two vessels linking up in space, calculated by NASA technicians? And these twenty miles were due to a simple breakdown which happened to increase our chances of recovery. For this to happen, a piston had to break in the engine of this ship which was sailing outside the normal shipping routes and its replacement had to take exactly the time necessary for the tanker's drift to coincide with the drift of our rubber ring.

To take this logic further, it should be pointed out that our chances were increased by the meeting happening at night, thus at the time when it was easiest to spot us, and that contrary to what usually happens on board a good number of ships of this type, there was a good lookout kept on the bridge.

All these coincidences, which seem like the outpourings of the overflowing imagination of a novelist, troubled us enough to lead to questions. And I don't think Alain Gouedard was joking when he said 'I've never had a mystical thought in my life, but it makes me wonder.' Olivier too kept repeating 'It's unbelievable', a remark which seemed to me to reveal his thoughts. Only, this rescue which can only be explained by elements of luck, seems to our five Cartesian minds a sufficiently disturbing reality to keep us well away from making the least admission.

Today, despite everything, we haven't changed our

views on this subject, but we're certainly more open with regard to believers. We've also become more open with regard to a society that we thought was led by money and lacking in human sense. From the very first day we had stated that there was little hope that a tanker, a Liberian one into the bargain, would come to our aid. Keep in mind the value of the cargo, affected by fluctuations on the stock exchange, which can be reduced by a half-day's delay, and also the final cost of the rescue manoeuvres, which not only use a great deal of fuel, but are a relatively delicate business in a raging sea, and could lead to damage or even loss of the cargo. That night, Captain Busetto demonstrated the meanness of this prejudiced view we had of a humanity ready to kill one another for a few pennies.

And then, as if to confirm my restored view of humanity, there were the tears at Roissy. A hundred or so people were waiting for us at Roissy Airport on Sunday, April 22. Our parents of course, our friends too, but also journalists, the curious, and the management of Timex and of RTL.

The airport authorities didn't allow this crowd to come as far as the gangway, as it's in the Customs-free zone. Just the RTL director and the chief editor were there, planted in the middle of the tiny disembarkation lounge, arms hanging, visibly not knowing what attitude to take. I was a bit cross with them because I wanted them to send Roger Zabel to meet me from the ship. During my two days in the United States I would have liked to have been guided, taken care of and not have responsibility for myself.

I intended to say this to them on that Sunday morning, but as I walked towards them the idea faded. I too didn't know what attitude to adopt. Should I shake their hands and ask them stupidly if they were 'all right'? Then, without even thinking about it, we hugged each other. It wasn't even a simple welcome, but the hug of a father and son. When my editor in chief tried to say a banal word of welcome, he found he couldn't speak, and tears shone in the corners of his eyes. He just managed to gasp 'Nicolas, it's too...!' and he couldn't finish his sentence. I'd practically forgotten that my companions were following me, I couldn't understand too well what was happening any more. I had a lump in my throat and a strong desire to cry too, but no tears came, and I couldn't speak at all. How should I react before these tears of joy, of emotion. It's *a priori* that a boss is someone with whom emotional relationships are limited to the payment of a salary. The masks fell there, in that airport hall; hierarchical relationships no longer existed. He was a man like any other, unable to hide his feelings. We could only exchange banalities on the moving walkway which led to the main hall. He'd put his dark glasses back on, but tiny sniffles which in other circumstances might be attributed to a bad cold still betrayed his emotion.

People are waving their arms about on the other side of the glass, some are clapping, and I can't even see the immigration officer who's wondering about the administrative value of the pass I'm offering him. I hardly hear him say 'And the Americans let you leave with *that*.' I look for my parents in the crowd. They're right over on the side by the door and we embrace across a barrier. I look for a cigarette more to put up a front than for any real need. Questions rain down, camera motors whir, and I'm already back at work replying to my colleagues from radio. A technician puts a headset on me so that I can broadcast direct on the 1 p.m. magazine programme on RTL. I'm preparing to reply to the question 'Did you despair?' with 'No, I didn't doubt that a search was underway' when I stop, for I suddenly remember that the Captain of the *Afran Dawn* had told us that he had received no alert.

That afternoon I ask my father and my friends from RTL what had been happening in Paris while we were adrift. In fact, nothing had been done to find us. The U.S. Coast Guard had never been warned of our disappearance or even of our delay. Of course my parents, my friends and the management of Timex and RTL had been worried for several days. So why didn't they alert the Coast Guard? The fact is, no one dared admit their apprehension so the responsibility of some calmed the fears of others. The RTL management replied to my father, who telephoned every day, that there was no reason to get worried; it was a sound boat, Alain Gliksman was a good sailor, and we'd probably been delayed a bit by the weather. After a few days of this kind of response, there was a rumour that *RTL-Timex* had been spotted off New York. It was already a week after our shipwreck when this news was put out. No one ever knew where this senseless information came from. In fact those responsible at RTL were as worried as our friends, but didn't dare tell my father, considering themselves responsible for my fate. They were wrong in this. My father knew that it was my decision and my decision alone to embark with Gliksman. It wasn't just a question of an exceptional story, but of a passion that needed to be satisfied. Then there was the phenomenon of the passing of responsibility. The RTL management passed it on to the directors of Timex France, and the directors of Timex France passed it on to Timex U.S.A., thinking they would act. In a nutshell, no one wanted to seem worried in front of the others. Furthermore, from a strict publicity angle, the two managements hesitated to have their joint venture end in general panic. Face had to be kept up, even if only for the sake of the media.

When simple questions were replaced by concern, there was no one at RTL who knew how to explain our delay. It might have been sufficient, if there'd been one single person in the editorial staff familiar enough with sailing to realize that if a boat leaves Bermuda on April 4 and still hasn't arrived in New York twelve days later, it's because she's in trouble. One evening the editor in chief rang our former sailing specialist on some pretext and at the end of the conversation, in the same way that one might say 'By the way, how's your wife?', asked him if it seemed to him reasonable to take thirteen days for the voyage from St George's Island to New York. His listener was surprised, to say the least, and replied that five days should be ample for such a voyage, or seven, in case of bad weather. But it's difficult for someone in charge of a press operation to admit that an attempt has failed.

So another night passed without any search being launched. It was nine days since we were wrecked. For seven nights already two people had been pacing the floor in a Paris apartment unable to sleep. In order not to upset my mother, my father claimed he had back pains; and my mother, while admitting that she was suffering from nightmares, didn't explain that I was the principal actor. Their distress had reached its peak but, like us in the raft, they had to wear a mask of confidence in order not to succumb to common despair. Which didn't stop my father from secretly spending several minutes on the telephone, two or three times a day, trying to get news of me. He even went as far as tracking down my woman colleague from *L'Express* on the scene of her current story to find out what information she'd been able to gather while waiting for us in New York. For this colleague had come to New York, waited three days, and left again, without concerning herself any more than that, not even attempting to get an explanation from the Coast Guard as to why we might be delayed!

During an editorial meeting on April 17 it was

decided that something must be done – but what? Strange as it may seem, for the staff of an outlying radio station, who are clever at tracking down in a quarter of an hour a secret restaurant in deepest Lozère where the Prime Minister is having lunch, no one knew how to proceed to find a reporter on the job. The former sailing specialist had to be recalled in order to begin the investigation. The Coast Guards were contacted in the middle of the day, but the management still couldn't resign themselves to launching an alert. Even after a discussion with the Coast Guard they again decided that Timex should take the responsibility. Another day and another night went by and then we were picked up. But as our rescue had not been announced in Paris, RTL finally decided on Wednesday the 18th to issue an alert to the American Coast Guard. After further communication with the Coast Guard officer there was a new dilemma: only sailors' families are capable of giving the green light for such a search to be undertaken.

This meant admitting to Mr. Angel, 'We're worried about your son. Take the first plane to New York and set the operation going.' If it wasn't Mr Angel, it would be Mrs Gliksman, Mr Gouedard or Mr Redkine, and the result would be the same: families in a panic and RTL responsible. Once more 'it was decided' to wait for the next day before resolving to use the final solution.

On Thursday the 19th the French press ran the story of the shipwreck of *Kriter IV*, Olivier de Kersauson's trimaran, while he was attempting to cross the Atlantic in less than twelve days. His port float broke during a storm and a Norwegian ship had picked him up two days earlier. Beneath the articles about this was a short sentence: 'Furthermore, there's still no news of *RTL-Timex* and her crew, who left Bermuda on April 4 to attempt the same record.'

This time RTL can't wait any longer. If Olivier de Kersauson's trimaran broke up, there's a strong chance that Gliksman's will have suffered damage. The daily press is beginning to talk. It's no longer possible to get Mr Angel to believe that there's no cause for alarm. A telephone message arrived just in time to save the RTL editorial staff from summoning my father: 'This is a U.S. Coast Guard officer. The crew of the *RTL-Timex* was picked up yesterday morning by a Liberian oil tanker. They had been adrift for nine days on a liferaft.'

The same evening my father treated the entire editorial staff to champagne, but remained astounded to have learned at the same moment that his son had been shipwrecked, had been adrift for nine days in the Atlantic ocean, and that he'd been saved.

In one way I'm happy that it turned out like this. If the trimaran's hull had been found while we were adrift, my father's heart might not have stood the strain. On the other hand, the discretion shown by our families, friends and those responsible for us, which prevented them from admitting their concern to themselves or to each other, might have lost us. Yet five months earlier Alain Colas' sad misadventure during the Route de Rhum was the same story. A search wasn't launched until a week after his last message. That time too no one dared admit their concern.

In the end it's a terrible vicious circle. Parents fear that their reaction might be exaggerated because, like all parents, they're afraid for their children and wait for those less directly concerned to get worried. But these people avoid communicating their distress to the family. Thus silence is maintained, everyone hides their feelings, and no constructive reaction can come from this attitude. In our case a search launched a week after our departure, let alone ten days, would certainly have failed. But later than this, even supposing planes had

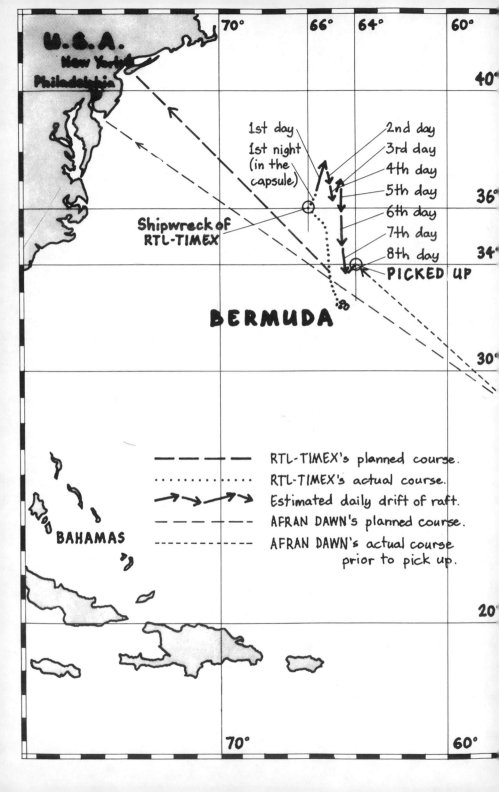

found our raft, I doubt if they'd have found us alive. Worry is a human feeling which is often well founded: it may be criminal not to dare to admit to it. A simple, positive analysis, based on the facts, can change a reaction of worry into a constructive plan of action.

Today my companions in this adventure are far from me. It took me a long time to get used to not having them by my side. So much so that the first time I awoke alone I felt helpless. I looked around for them, I missed them. I needed to hear Alain's 'Great' and Denis's 'Superb'... but then we went back to our respective occupations. Alain and Denis Gliksman are sailing on new boats – not necessarily monohulls. Olivier and Alain continue their search for craft in which to participate in more and more races on the high seas.

As for me, I'm happy to write about their exploits from my office on the Rue Bayard, while waiting feverishly for my holidays to again go sailing.

We haven't broken the link with the sea. On the contrary, we have some revenge to take. Besides, we feel that our quota of bad luck must have been entirely used up, which feeling authorizes us to practically cross the Place de la Concorde with our eyes closed. Despite which we're aware from now on that it's stupid to think that such things 'only happen to other people', and we'll incorporate significant modifications to the survival equipment when we undertake future passages.

For Alain Gliksman, even more than for the rest of us, a race has begun which has nothing in common with those across the Atlantic. It has to do with the future of trimarans and the improvement of so-called liferafts. The trimaran is still in the stone age: it must survive, but evolve. Just because there have been a series of accidents between the end of 1978 and the beginning of 1979 doesn't mean that these great seabirds must die. On the contrary it should push marine designers to deepen their researches in order to increase their safety. This is the first round in this fight which Alain has undertaken. For the second, we're all five of us concerned, and all five of us will act so that castaways need no longer be passive 'things' who can only hope, with no chance of helping in their fate.

9

So That Ships Don't Turn Up Too Late in Future

I've tried hard to give an exact account of the different episodes of our shipwreck and the days that followed without artifice and in the most direct manner. But I think this story would be incomplete if it didn't include a search for the lessons to be drawn from it. Sometimes we found our courage again in moments of deepest despair by remembering the experiences of other castaways, both voluntary (Bombard) and involuntary (the Robertson family). Their response in matters of survival often saved us from making mistakes, or on the other hand led us to try things we wouldn't necessarily have thought of.

As a journalist I'm content to make remarks and suggestions. I don't claim to supplant marine architects, designers of survival gear or experts in nutrition. But I do think that our misadventure gives me the right to raise certain points. Obviously most of the problems raised were debated among us all. But quite often the flagrant evidence of some point produced no answer.

RTL-Timex's **wreck: could the capsize have been avoided?**

There are three ways of fighting a gale: reducing sail to a storm jib, drifting under bare poles, and flight.

Three hours before the trimaran's capsize, we had set a storm jib. That is, with the tiny storm jib and a lee helm, we drifted with the wind abeam and heading into the waves. But this mode proved too dangerous for the boat which received powerful blows as she fell into troughs we estimated as ten to twelve metres deep. The hull and floats struck the water surface more and more brutally and began to show signs of fatigue, threatening to damage the trimaran's structure. After some hours, the leeward float began digging deeper and deeper under the water. Several strokes of the pump were enough to bring it back up, but if refilled very rapidly. This led Gliksman to decide to take up our course again, negotiating each wave to protect the boat as we made headway. To obtain this result, we unrolled two or three square metres of staysail, while keeping up the storm jib. The boat was a lot easier to handle with this extra canvas. The technique consisted of climbing the wave with it on the bow quarter, then going down away from the wind in order to gain speed and tackle the next wave with greater impetus. The method was good, but very trying for the helmsman who had to keep accurately calculating his angle of attack. Since the weather continued to worsen, Gliksman decided to use the safest method, which would spare the crew: bare poles, no canvas, and a sea anchor to hold the boat into the waves. This is what we were preparing to do when a crossing wave lifted up the float when it was already out of the water at the crest of another wave, and turned us over without a thing we could do about it.

So would flight have been a good solution? Certainly not, if I'm to believe Alain Gliksman's analysis;

the operation is much too risky with a trimaran. As its name suggests, flight consists of running before the wind and waves, often while slowing down the boat's speed. A heavy line is thrown into the water to slow the boat down from the stern, like a trawl net. But a too-fast trimaran is in danger of overtaking a wave, stalling and pitchpoling over her bows. We can sum up by saying that nothing could be done, for you can't fight an exceptional wave. A monohull yacht would doubtless have been turned over in the same way, but of course her heavy keel would have righted her afterwards, which isn't the case for a trimaran.

Should some system for righting trimarans be devised? Yacht designers should think about this, and Gliksman isn't the only one to hope they'll come up with a rapid solution.

Lifejackets and safety lines

To be honest we must criticize ourselves, as we didn't take the precaution of wearing lifejackets and safety harnesses, though the boat was well provided with them. Either a skipper orders the wearing of lifejackets with no arguments, or he leaves it up to his crew. If he decides not to wear one it's difficult to persuade his crew to do so, a reaction most often due to vanity. As for personal lifelines, in our case it's certain that the helmsman, Olivier as it happened, might have been trapped under the hull after the capsize if he'd been attached to the boat by a safety line. On the other hand, he'd have had less trouble getting back on board if he'd been wearing a lifejacket, weighed down as he was by his gear.

Liferaft stowage

It's obviously impossible to generalize about this. As far as we were concerned, and by extension on a great number of other trimarans, the cockpit cannot be considered a good place any more. Positioning the raft on deck at the foot of the mast, as on a monohull, reduces the chance of recovering it in case of capsize to one in ten. On the other hand, if it could be fixed to the float crossbeams the risk of its being trapped practically disappears. Using a more costly method, it would be possible to fix it to a frame off the stern. Nothing further could then hinder its launching, even if the hull were overturned.

Finally there's the undoubtedly wisest and most efficient solution: fix the raft to the side of the hull. The creator of this technique, the careful Phil Weld, has already experimented with it against his will! Since two precautions are better than one, his trimaran *Rogue Wave* is currently equipped with a liferaft to starboard and a sailing dinghy to port.

Survival capsule gear

When we got into this miniature grotto, it was already night and our watertight torches failed us completely. But light is primordial, as much for getting one's bearings, finding gear, doing small jobs, etc as for removing the terror of the dark. Without any doubt the most successful method, given the impossibility of recovering anything from water filled cabins, would be to have a watertight bag filled with minimum survival gear (sweaters, oilskin overalls, knife, tools, navigation instruments, provisions and of course a torch). Don't forget that even if in our case it didn't work as foreseen by the designer, the survival capsule should eliminate the need to embark in the liferaft.

The unsinkability of an upturned trimaran

It seems that in our case, once the hull was overturned,

she began to sink rapidly, dragged down by her water-logged float; if this had met our expectations, we could have stayed in the survival capsule. To the extent that her structure is undamaged, a multihull will always make a better raft than any rubber dinghy. In any case it's always better to have a plank of wood under your behind than a bit of rubber tube. Besides, a big wreck will always be easier to spot than a little dinghy. The ideal method would be to fill the floats with expanded polystyrene foam or furnish them with an inflatable rubber tube in case they get damaged. It's up to the designers to work it out in detail.

General problems we became aware of during our stay in the raft

ADVANCE precautions! If the authorities are unable to classify types of liferafts differently from the current recommendations, for reasons unknown to the public, the user must at the very least, and from the moment of purchase, be able to know what's in the appliance so that he can himself remedy the intolerable defects which are detailed in the following pages. Remember that lifesaving appliances are statutory [in some countries], and expensive. So it seems logical that the buyer of such a costly item should at least be able to supervise the organization of his future rescue himself, and not die an idiot! One solution would obviously be to have extra components or units, designed to include anything that could improve or prolong the chances of survival. I'm not claiming that the following is an exhaustive list, but it must be nearly so, taking into account our shipwreck and various other stories of the same kind which I've heard.

So why not, as Sir Francis Chichester did, place watertight bags with supplies appropriate to the region of the voyage at strategic points around the yacht,

notably in the survival area, containing:
– warm undergarments of the 'polar suit' type
– woollen socks and sweaters
– oilskin overalls
– torches and spare batteries
– a knife of the Opinel type*
– dried fruit and tubes of condensed milk
– strong fishing tackle
– spare compass
– Pilot Charts (showing prevailing wind directions, currents, shipping routes, etc)
– flares
– small coils of line

Conclusions from the period we were adrift in the liferaft

Our two enemies were indisputably the cold and the wet. But if it seemed easy to us to suggest remedies for the defects of the 'bib' and its gear, it seemed extremely difficult to state how we could have struggled effectively against these two scourges. Leaving aside the problem of the watertightness of the canopy, which I'll come back to, it seemed unlikely that anyone could stay perfectly dry in as rough seas as we were roaming in for those nine days. Despite what one might think, oilskin overalls are not the best solution. They're generally designed to be watertight, so have no holes water can run out of. Now they are in fact not watertight, despite all the precautions taken in the design of the cuffs, trouser bottoms and neckband. Water will always find a way in and after a time form a disagreeable pool beneath the buttocks. This water will then make the

*Opinel is a trademark for a folding knife with a wooden handle, issued to the French Army and Navy; it is easy to hold, strong, stainless steel and keeps its edge.

wearer cold, and above all, after a few days painfully sore. Until manufacturers have found the answer to this, it's better to be warm if one's got to be wet. Gliksman was wearing three woollen sweaters and was the only one not to suffer from the cold because wool warms even when wet, unlike synthetic fabrics. So we advocate woollen sweaters and socks.

We didn't really have to suffer from hunger or thirst. We were well supplied with water and the North Atlantic climate didn't dehydrate us. Obviously the problem is reversed in the tropics. But in this type of experience, one evil replaces another! As for hunger, luckily we weren't adrift long enough for us to suffer from this. All the while there are survival rations, vitamin biscuits and glucose, the body will tick over slowly. Vitamin biscuits perfectly fulfill their function, but lack taste. Glucose tablets are an important source of calories for fighting the cold, but are very sickly to eat. We could often have wished to boost our morale with something with a bit of taste to it.

In conclusion, everything that can be saved from the ship will be appreciated, particularly fresh or dried fruit, chocolate, tubes of condensed milk, for all these high-energy foods also taste good. We weren't able to try plankton, since our plankton net was also our sea anchor and it treacherously left us before we were able to test its effectiveness. The seaweed I tried on the penultimate day didn't taste of anything much other than iodine, and I wonder if it has any nutritional value.

If we'd been able to catch the dorado which escorted us during our whole time adrift, this would have made a big difference. Unfortunately the fishing lines were ridiculously weak; there were three hooks but no lures, and only the bottom end of the line was supplied, with no reel of fishing line to tie it to. Also we had nothing to kill the fish with having landed them.

Our nine days' survival didn't push us to the limit, but if it had continued for as long again we would have needed solutions that our gear couldn't provide. On the other hand, our adventure took place in the North Atlantic: it would have been a different matter in the tropics and with a calm sea.

The liferaft

For nine days we were forced to drift and wait for help, without being able to aid providence to save us. This impotence is trying, for we would have liked to be able to negotiate the waves (which might have prevented our overturning) and to choose to remain near the site of the wreck or to try to reach the coast. Our 'Bombard' Angevinière* is quite round, so by definition has neither bow nor stern, which must give it greater stability but didn't prevent us from having to fight every minute not to be overturned. Certainly the weather conditions were exceptionally bad, but the roundness of the raft seemed to us to have no evident usefulness. We also saw that the chances of getting picked up by a ship are slim. For this to be possible, an S.O.S. must be picked up and help arrive before the liferaft has drifted too far away. All of which leads us to conclude that rafts must be made navigable.

Furthermore the craft from which today's liferafts are derived, Dr Bombard's famous *Hérétique*, was oblong with a bow, a stern, a rudder and a small sail. Why have the responsible authorities persisted in favouring round craft for twenty-five years, on the pretext that they're more stable? It's been said for several

---

*Dr Alain Bombard lent his name to the Société Angeviniére some fifteen years ago, but that doesn't go so far as to mean that all the inflatable rafts manufactured by that company are identical to the one in which he crossed the Atlantic – *L'Hérétique*. On the contrary, up to the time of our shipwreck, all liferafts were round or hexagonal, and impossible to navigate.

years that 'dynamic' rafts will replace so-called 'static' ones. I hope our story will weigh the balance so that the generation of 'idiot rafts' will disappear. Be that as it may, and to stay with existing rafts, simple modifications could greatly improve the chances of survival.

Stability: our Angevinière was endowed with two water pockets to reduce the risk of overturning. Rubber pockets attached underneath the raft act as drags when full of water, making it less easily tipped up and holding it down onto the water. It is obvious that in our case they didn't work. Should they be larger to make them more effective in bad weather? The designers can judge for themselves!

The sea anchor: the sea anchor (drogue) and its line are vital survival gear and should prevent the raft from drifting too far from the position of the wreck. Furthermore, it enabled us to maintain the raft's direction in relation to the waves, and by extension to help keep our balance. It seemed to us that without it the raft tended to take off with a crest and get tumbled into a trough. So, since we couldn't sail, it prevented us from playing at being a cork. The first sea anchor lasted four days – only four days because its warp was the size of a telephone cord, and looked like plastic string for wrapping presents with. We replaced the sea anchor three times with whatever we could find, and three times it broke. We had to double up the line to get enough strength. Without any doubt, this together with the watertightness of the canopy was the problem that strained us most physically and morally. It's inconceivable that this vital item should be too small. And it isn't a question of a design problem, of delicate techniques... could it be simply a question of saving money?

Watertightness: a vital problem. If we'd been able to keep dry, we'd have suffered a lot less from the cold and would thus have been able to hold out longer in much better conditions. The canopy flaps are closed at three points: glued at the top, hooked in the middle and at the bottom. The overlap is two or three centimetres. Waves have no trouble getting in and moreover their repeated attacks stretch the fabric so that the flaps don't overlap anymore. Three-quarters of our physical suffering came from this lack of watertightness: hence the importance that should be given to it. Could it be again to save money that the manufacturer didn't provide a greater degree of overlap (by ten or twenty centimetres for example)? And why wasn't a proper method of closure provided? A zip would obviously be efficient, but dangerous in the event of a sudden evacuation. Strips of Velcro are the key to this problem. To make a really watertight closure, a provision to reduce the need for frequent opening also needs to be made. One's head must be shoved out to make a proper observation, sometimes even the whole torso. If four plastic portholes were incorporated into each of the four sides of the canopy this problem would be solved.

Fishing: we weren't forced to fish, but we were nonetheless able to gauge the inadequacy of the gear provided. It's the truth that when Gliksman made his report to the American Coast Guard they were of the opinion that this gear was provided to keep the castaways busy, rather than to actually supply their needs! In fact, with the worthy sentiment of keeping us in good health, someone had decided that we ran the risk of poisoning ourselves by eating the wrong kind of fish. Yet all we saw were innocent dorado, which have an excellent reputation for edibility. To my knowledge, only one fish is supposed to be poisonous: the trigger-fish, which prefers tropical seas. Its body is a fat oval shape, its enormous head takes up a third of its size, while its powerful teeth are less dangerous than the dorsal spurs which contain the poison. So we would have preferred to have found good strong lines (stainless steel wire for example) with fair-sized hooks, soldered to suitable lures for the kind of fish likely to be encountered. Even better would be a boathook or harpoon, for the fish are close at hand and if they choose not to take the lure they could then be caught with a bit of skill and landed in the 'bib'. Equally one needs to be provided with a strong sharp knife to cut short their threshing in the bottom of the craft, as they're extremely lively. Don't forget that it is now an established fact that the fluid from the spine of a fish can make up for a lack of water for a time.

Water: we didn't have a problem with this. The two jerry cans of twenty litres each were ample, and the nine litres in the tins packed in the raft gave us an appreciable margin. On the other hand the packing of these tins needs improvement, not to say total change. There was no way provided of closing a tin once it had been opened, which forces the consumption of the whole tin, since there's no way to keep it. Why not provide plastic containers with replaceable caps?

There's also a problem with rainwater, even though the principle of capturing water falling on the canopy, via a small gutter connected to a tube, is basically sound. Even on condition that you've got the small cup provided with the original gear, the boon of a shower lasts the time it takes to drink two mouthfuls of water at the most.

Finally, this war of experts on whether it is dangerous or not to drink seawater must be settled. In 1953

Dr Alain Bombard demonstrated that the body survives longer by alternating the drinking of fresh and sea water; however, the latter must not exceed six days. Since then other specialists have added to the controversy to the extent that no one knows what's good or bad! Personally, if I were to be confronted with the problem of thirst, between dying from dehydration and trying sea water, regardless of the consequences I would choose the second solution.

Comfort: you know when you get into a liferaft that you're not about to begin a pleasure cruise. But is that a reason to fail to equip the craft in the best and most comfortable way, thereby rendering its use more logical? We'd discovered the first problem within ten minutes of embarking: there was no way to prevent the loss of gear if we overturned. The handholds provided in the bottom and round the circumference of the raft could be excellent places of attachment if they were fitted with small loops of cord. If we hadn't had our anorak cords, our jerry cans would have been lost overboard immediately. It must also be remembered that some objects, for example round ones, are almost impossible to tie down. Wouldn't it be possible to simply provide sealed pockets on the floats? The bottom of the liferaft is also inflated and this is perfect for insulation from the cold and the vicious attacks of some fish. But after a long stay, this soft surface becomes a virtual bed of nails. Moreover, the rolls are similar to those of an air mattress and sometimes make it impossibly difficult to bail. A flexible lattice floor would permanently avoid contact with the water and maybe even enable us to lift ourselves up from time to time. For, after twenty-four hours, having to live seated or lying is no longer tolerable. After this lapse of time, cramps multiply and the leg muscles won't work any more, which adds to general weakening. Anyway, if the major part of the time must be spent in a sitting position, it certainly wouldn't be a totally superfluous luxury to be able to slip an inflatable cushion underneath one's fleshy parts, or between the back and the raft tubes.

To conclude, there's one detail whose importance may seem excessive when one hasn't been in this situation, and that is the need for something to do. On the rare times when we were inactive, we regretted not having a pack of cards or some similar pastime to keep our hands busy and thereby avoid letting dark thoughts stir.

Rescue
The fact that six ships passed near us and only one saw us reveals the gravity of this problem. Recovery must be considered from two angles: night and day. In the daytime we must accept that just because we can see a ship doesn't mean that her crew can make us out. A liferaft disappears among the waves like a tiny cork. While we may be motivated to scrutinize the whole surface of the ocean, the duty officer on a ship can content himself with looking straight ahead, and often it's even the radar that's doing this. But although radar scans through 360°, a liferaft is very low in the water, lost among the waves, and doesn't send back a good echo. Thus if it isn't directly on the ship's course there is little chance that it will attract the attention of the officers or crew, or be perceived on the radar screen.

Hand flares, either burning or smoke types, have a very limited range since they must be held at arm's length at a height which never exceeds 2.50 metres above the water. When the wave troughs are ten or twelve metres deep, there's little hope of being spotted by a ship except during the brief moments when one's on the crest of a wave. Even in a calm sea it seems that the chance of being picked up by day must be markedly less with hand flares than with smoke flares. But smoke flares are totally useless when the wind's blowing at 30 or 40 knots because instead of rising up, the smoke is beaten down onto the water. So, they must be equipped with rockets and parachutes so that they can go off at a height and then fall trailing smoke.

Rocket flares are much more useful, since they rise to a height of 80 metres before going off, but the flare only lasts a short time (about five seconds). The most perfect distress signal is a parachute flare which rises to 180 metres and burns for the 30 seconds of its fall. But by day these light signals will always remain a luminous spot in the immensity of the ocean, while at night their bright light makes a large streak in the darkness. An officer who notices a bright spot twenty miles off his course for the space of two seconds might think he was seeing things, but at night, he wouldn't doubt his sight. By day, if the sun's out, a signalling mirror is an excellent method of attracting attention, but it takes practice to use it when you need it without losing precious seconds. There remains the classic reflex of the castaway, which consists of waving clothes about. This may seem laughable, but could be one of the best methods: an orange oilskin or an aluminium sheet make beautiful streaks of colour in the middle of the blue-green and white of the ocean. As for being spotted by a plane that isn't even looking for you, this idea is just a hopeful dream. I checked during my return flight to Europe. Even a large ship is impossible to detect among the white crests of big waves.

Together with Alain Gliksman, we devised the following method: one must have a balloon inflated with lighter-than-air gas and tied to the raft. This would rise to a hundred or so metres and permanently show our position. Its retaining cable could possibly be used as an aerial for a distress beacon. Transmitting distress beacons should be the surest method of rescue, but they're not powerful enough and only transmit on 2182 kHz, the maritime band frequency reserved for this type of signal. It's obvious that ships aren't constantly listening in on this frequency. It would take an extraordinary stroke of luck for the operator to happen to be listening in on 2181 at the precise moment when the ship passed within range of the transmission. The most useful radio is not authorized by the P.T.T*. It consists of a powerful beacon transmitting on civil airline frequencies. A simple continuous note transmitted for forty-eight hours would undoubtedly be picked up by an airliner. To extend transmission time, a completely different type of battery from those currently used must be provided; ordinary batteries are inadequate. I suppose that cost alone prevents the inclusion of solar cells or more powerful seawater batteries in the basic specification.

Finally, and this will be my last point, would a notice giving instructions for the use of the raft have weighed too much? Of course castaways always find new ways of surviving, but a little leaflet would be welcome, even if only for the reading matter it provided. It might contain a description of the raft, an inventory of the gear on board, recommendations with regard to weather, the principles of survival (fishing, drinking, exercise), ideas on recovery.

On our arrival in France, Alain Gliksman was eager to point out the most serious gaps, or improvements, to be made to our liferaft and its gear. From the moment we embarked in the 'bib' he hadn't disguised his anger.

---

*The P.T.T. (Poste, Télégraphes, Téléphones) which in France is the authority which governs radio transmissions and equipment.

Thus he presented the list I've just run through in a few pages, with vehemence. Some people might find it hard to understand our demands, which are also those of Alain, Olivier and Denis. 'How could we accuse the people who designed, built and sold the appliance which saved our lives?' Well, I'll reply to anyone who asks this question with two points:

Olivier was dying of cold and the lack of protection the raft offered against the weather. Alain was next on the list, and although Alain Gliksman, his son Denis and I could have survived longer, we had no way of reaching land, nor could we fish to stay alive while we awaited our hypothetical rescue. So, yes, the rubber of our raft stayed inflated and we went on floating till a ship arrived. But if this ship hadn't suffered a mechanical breakdown two days earlier, we'd never have encountered her and I know I would never have been able to write this book.

Anyway, just because one's life has been saved, must one forget? Just because we were picked up, does this mean others won't be shipwrecked one day and find themselves on a rubber raft?

We wanted to inform the merchants of survival so that ships don't turn up too late in future!

Plan de la Tour
May 22, 1979

10

One Year Later

Written by the author for the English edition

I n France, the wreck of *RTL-Timex* brought about an
enormous controversy over survival equipment. The
drama of the 1979 Fastnet Race a few months later
pushed this argument beyond French borders.

As Gliksman, Redkine, Gouedard and I had
wished, the publication of this book forced the people
concerned to react. Those whom I called 'merchants of
survival' at the end of the last chapter finally awoke
from their lethargy and understood that the growing
awareness of navigators with regard to safety and survival meant that they could no longer rest on their
laurels – to the extent that they had any. So we have
partially accomplished our aims, and all things considered our shipwreck wasn't in vain.

If I had to list the positive repercussions that followed the telling of our misadventure, I would sum-
marise them with three points:

The growing awareness of mariners of all kinds,
whether professional skippers, delivery crews, Sunday
sailors or fishermen (perhaps the most concerned).

The growing awareness of survival equipment manufacturers, with, it must be acknowledged, the Société Angevinière which made the raft on which we suffered, in the foremost position.

The growing awareness of the French maritime authorities. Previously immune to the idea of revising their categories of rafts, they are now studying the possibility of allowing on board 'dynamic' steerable rafts to replace the existing 'static' types.

For these reasons it seems appropriate to make some amendments to Chapter 9, 'So That Ships Don't Turn Up Too Late in Future'.

Precautions before making use of the liferaft

From now on, in France, anyone buying a liferaft can demand to be present when it is packed, in order to know what has been put in the container. Equally, they can add personal items, as far as space allows. (These could be extra distress flares, or a bottle of good Scotch.) The same possibility is open to the owner of a liferaft at the time of the compulsory annual inspection.

To be added to the list of contents for the survival bags: a press (for squeezing the juices out of fish); small cans of fruit juice; muesli (a mixture of cereal, raisins etc); separate lids or caps for containers; sunglasses and a hat (for tropical waters).

The raft

In September 1979 I personally took part in a survival experiment in the Mediterranean (voluntary this time!) on a 'dynamic' navigable raft. As a result of this I can state that navigable rafts are not a universal panacea. Certainly they can be sailed, and in a relatively precise direction, but in their present form not every sailor would be capable of using them. Nevertheless they could improve by 80 per cent the chances of survival of those cast adrift when ocean racing: they can obviously be considered skilled sailors.

But such a device in the hands of the inexperienced could make search operations more difficult, for such a raft would distance itself more rapidly from the position estimated for the wreck by rescuers, and not necessarily in the direction of land or of shipping routes. Still, it must be acknowledged that some equipment manufacturers have made a laudable effort, which should be pursued until such a device can be entrusted to all.

Stability
Some manufacturers have added an extra water pocket, but the results are still inconclusive.

The drogue or sea anchor
The three principal French makers (Angevinière, Zodiac, Plastimo) have reinforced the sea anchor gear: the thickness of the line has been doubled, and a swivel put between the end of the warp and the cords going to the edge of the 'parachute' so that the lines do not get twisted.

Watertightness
Some raft makers have modified the system for closing the canopy. The flaps have been lengthened on one side, and there is an overlapping double closing. Underneath is a zipper which goes halfway up; above and over this is a flap which rolls down from the top and is closed with buttons. This allows one's head to be outside, and is practical since very often the water comes in only at the bottom. The arrangement is more efficient, but unfortunately it still remains to be tested.

Search and rescue
In the space of one year technology has evolved with

great speed. Several electronics companies in France now sell self-contained buoys which transmit on the civil aviation frequencies (145 MHz).

As a point of interest, officials of the French airline pilots' association have told me that they 'amused themselves' calculating the number of planes that flew over the zone of our shipwreck, and thus could possibly have picked up our distress call if we had possessed such a beacon. During the nine days we were adrift, two thousand flights could have caught our appeals... I hardly feel this needs comment!

A year has gone by, the horizons of survival at sea are opening up, and I have the impression now that ships will not always arrive too late. But the improvement in the conditions of survival shouldn't stop there. That is my wish, and that of my companions.

As a matter of fact... for those who are interested, Gliksman, Denis, Alain, Olivier and I are still sailing and with still more pleasure.

JOHN W. FAWCETT, III

CONSUL HONORAIRE DE FRANCE
À PHILADELPHIE

THREE PARKWAY
PHILADELPHIA, PA. 19102
TEL: (215) LO 3-0650

LAISSER PASSER

Nom: ANGEL, Yves-Nicholas

Nationalité: Française

Né: le 29-11-1954

A: Neuilly-sur-Seine, France

Je, soussigne, JOHN W. FAWCETT, III, consul de France à Philadelphie,
certifie que Monsieur ANGEL a perdu son passeport au cours d'un
nauffrage.

Monsieur ANGEL est de nationalité française.

Fawcett, III
de France à Philadelphie

Thanks

To CAPTAIN GIOVANNI BUSETTO and the crew of the *Afran Dawn*, for reasons that need no explanation.

To ROGER ZABEL, friend rather than colleague, for his help before, during and after.

To VINCENT DUVIVIER who helped me put my ideas in order without imposing his own!

To J.W. FAWCETT III, Honorary French Consul in Philadelphia, and his wife, for their welcome.

To LIZA DIAZ and her mother ALEXANDRA for their smiles at our arrival and their tears at our departure for the United States.

To AIR FRANCE who altered their flight plans to get us back to our friends quicker.

Lastly, to the Paris restaurant LA GAULOISE which provided our first French meal worthy of the name.